HUMAN IMPERFECTION

While We Were Sinners Christ Died for Us

EDWARD D. ANDREWS

HUMAN IMPERFECTION

While We Were Sinners Christ Died for Us

Edward D. Andrews

Christian Publishing House
Cambridge, Ohio

Copyright © 2017, 2025 Edward D. Andrews

All rights reserved. Except for brief quotations in articles, other publications, book reviews, and blogs, no part of this book may be reproduced in any manner without prior written permission from the publishers. For information, write, support@christianpublishers.org

Unless otherwise stated, Scripture quotations are from Updated American Standard Version (UASV) Copyright © 2022 by Christian Publishing House

HUMAN IMPERFECTION: While We Were Sinners Christ Died for Us by Edward D. Andrews

ISBN-10: 1945757558

ISBN-13: 978-1945757556

Table of Contents

Preface 7

Introduction 9

CHAPTER 1 The Image of God and the Creation of Humanity: Dignity, Purpose, and Moral Agency 11

CHAPTER 2 The Fall of Man: From Perfection to Imperfection in Eden 20

CHAPTER 3 Exploring the Depth of Human Sinfulness: Heart, Mind, and Will Under Corruption 26

CHAPTER 4 The Nature and Consequences of Sin: Death, Corruption, and Divine Justice 33

CHAPTER 5 Why Suffering Exists in God's Creation: Jehovah's Answer to Eden and Job 39

CHAPTER 6 Regaining Control: The Mind of Christ and Biblical Thinking 47

CHAPTER 7 Foreknowledge: God's Insight into the Future and the Question of Molinism 53

CHAPTER 8 Navigating Life with Free Will: Freedom Under Jehovah's Sovereignty 59

CHAPTER 9 The Guidance of the Holy Spirit in Christian Life 64

CHAPTER 10 God's Purpose for Humanity and Earth 72

CHAPTER 11 Christ's Sacrifice: The Ultimate Hope for Fallen Humanity 79

CHAPTER 12 Salvation as a Path and Journey with the Heavenly Hope and the Earthly Hope 85

CHAPTER 13 Living in Anticipation: Preparing for the New Heavens and Earth 93

CHAPTER 14 Embracing Our Imperfection, Holding onto Hope 100

CHAPTER 15 Receiving the Benefit of Christ's Death: Repentance, Baptism, and the Life of Obedient Faith 106

CHAPTER 16 Death, Resurrection, and Judgment: What Scripture Actually Promises to Imperfect Humans 112

Other Books by Edward D. Andrews 118

Preface

In the vast expanse of human history, few topics have evoked as much contemplation, debate, and introspection as our understanding of ourselves in relation to the Divine. At the heart of this exploration lies a paradox: we are, as Scripture attests, meticulously crafted in the very image of God—yet, we grapple daily with imperfections that seem to defy this divine lineage. How did we come to this crossroad of celestial origin and earthly frailty?

"HUMAN IMPERFECTION: While We Were Sinners Christ Died For Us" seeks not just to answer this question but to journey with the reader through the tapestry of biblical texts, unearthing the roots of our human condition, the profound implications of our choices, and the overarching sovereignty of God in the midst of it all.

The pages that follow are more than a theological exposition; they are a pilgrimage. A pilgrimage through the annals of Scripture, from the pristine Garden of Eden to the tumultuous landscapes of a world yearning for redemption. Along the way, we'll confront challenging concepts—like the interplay between God's foreknowledge and human free will—and discover the depth of God's love, so profound that while we were entrenched in sin, Christ offered Himself for our salvation.

It's my prayer that as you journey through this book, you'll not only gain a deeper understanding of the nuances of our human imperfection but also embrace the resounding hope and redemption available to us all. This is not just a chronicle of humanity's fall but a testament to God's unyielding grace and the transformative power of Christ's sacrifice.

Edward D. Andrews

May you be enriched, challenged, and ultimately drawn closer to God's heart as you delve into the intricacies of our shared human story, and the divine love that seeks to redeem it.

Edward D. Andrews

Author of 220+ books and Chief Translator of the Updated American Standard Version

Introduction

From the dawn of human existence, our story has been punctuated with moments of brilliance and shadows of failings. As beings created in the divine image of God, we've been entrusted with an incredible legacy. Yet, the imperfections that have woven themselves into our very essence raise questions that are as ancient as they are pertinent: What led us down this path of dichotomy, where the divine and the flawed coexist within us? And where does our hope lie in this intricate dance between our heavenly heritage and earthly inclinations?

This book isn't just an academic endeavor or a mere compilation of biblical exegesis. Instead, it's an invitation—a call to journey deeper into the heart of our shared human experience. Through its chapters, we will traverse the landscapes of ancient Scripture, gleaning insights from the lives of those who walked before us. We will witness firsthand the transformative power of God's Word, shining a light on the corners of our humanity that are often shrouded in mystery.

The nature of sin, the profound impact of the fall, and the inherent bent of the human heart towards wrongdoing are themes that have been explored across ages. Yet, in our exploration, we'll seek fresh perspectives, drawing from the wellspring of Scripture and looking through the lens of God's eternal wisdom. We'll grapple with complex theological concepts, yet always with an aim to draw practical, life-affirming lessons for our contemporary world.

But beyond the exploration of our flaws and the intricacies of sin lies a beacon of hope. A hope anchored in the very essence of the Gospel—the redemptive work of Christ on our behalf. As we delve deeper into understanding our imperfections, we'll also discover the boundless love and grace that God extends, drawing us back to Him, time and time again.

So, as we embark on this expedition together, I encourage you to approach the pages that follow with an open heart and a seeker's curiosity. Let's together unearth the layers of our human story, always with an eye on the redemptive horizon that God promises.

Let the journey begin.

CHAPTER 1 The Image of God and the Creation of Humanity: Dignity, Purpose, and Moral Agency

The Biblical Account of Humanity's Origin

Genesis presents humanity's beginning as a purposeful act of Jehovah, not an accident of nature or a product of competing deities. The text moves from the forming of environments to the filling of those environments with life, and then reaches a peak when God creates human beings. This literary progression is not mere artistry; it communicates that mankind is placed within a prepared world and given an assigned role. Humanity is not simply another creature alongside others but is introduced as the one creature made to represent God's interests in the earthly realm.

Genesis 1:26–27 records the divine intention: "Let us make man in our image, according to our likeness." The historical-grammatical reading takes these words as the Creator's deliberate decision to fashion a being who, unlike animals, is equipped for moral reasoning, relational responsibility, and accountable dominion. The point is not that God has a human body. Scripture elsewhere affirms that God is spirit. The "image" is therefore functional and moral, expressed in how humans think, choose, love, govern, create, communicate, and worship.

Genesis 2 complements Genesis 1 by describing mankind's creation with a different angle: God formed the man from the dust of the ground and breathed into his nostrils the breath of life, and the man became "a living soul." The language is plain and concrete. Man is not described as receiving an immortal, conscious entity that lives inside him. Rather, the person becomes a living soul when the material body is animated by life from God. This foundation matters because it shapes how Scripture speaks of life, death, accountability, and redemption across the rest of the Bible.

What It Means to Be Made in God's Image

Image and Likeness as Representative Rule

The immediate context in Genesis 1 ties God's image to mankind's commission: "let them have dominion." The image is connected to representative rule under God. Humans are commissioned to govern the earth in a way that reflects God's righteous standards. Dominion is not permission for cruelty or exploitation. It is stewardship under the Creator, exercised in a manner consistent with His character—orderly, wise, life-supporting, and morally governed.

This also explains why Scripture treats human life as uniquely weighty. Later, Genesis 9 grounds the prohibition of murder in the reality that man is made in God's image. That argument does not depend on human usefulness, health, strength, age, social status, or intelligence. It depends on what humanity is by creation: an image-bearer accountable to God.

Rationality, Conscience, and Moral Accountability

Humans are made to understand, evaluate, and choose. Genesis assumes this from the start: Adam is given a command, meaning he can comprehend moral instruction. He is also given work, meaning he can plan and execute purposeful action. He is given relationships, meaning he can communicate, love, and covenant. These features are not peripheral; they reveal the kind of creature man is.

The image of God includes the capacity for conscience. Even after the fall, Scripture repeatedly appeals to human responsibility: "choose," "turn," "repent," "listen," "obey." These are not empty words. Jehovah's commands assume moral agency, even in a fallen world. Human sinfulness affects perception and desire, but Scripture still addresses people as accountable persons who can respond to truth.

Relational Capacity and Covenant Responsibility

Genesis shows that man is not designed for isolation. "It is not good for the man to be alone" is not a comment about emotional preference but about created design. Humans are built for relationships that carry moral obligations: marriage, family, community, worship, and service. Being made in God's image includes the ability to know God, speak to Him, and live under His moral government.

This relational dimension also implies that the image of God is not merely individual. God created mankind as a plurality—male and female—so that human life would immediately reflect relational life. The first human society begins in a marriage covenant, and that covenant becomes the foundational context for multiplying, teaching, working, and worshiping.

Holiness and the Call to Reflect God's Character

Being made in God's image is not limited to capacities; it also includes a moral calling. In the New Testament, Christians are described as being "renewed" in knowledge and righteousness. This renewal language shows that the image has ethical content. God intends human beings to live in truth, purity, love, justice, and faithfulness. When humans lie, exploit, commit violence, or worship idols, they do not cease being human; they deface what they were meant to display.

This is why Scripture can speak both of human dignity and human guilt without contradiction. Dignity is rooted in creation. Guilt is rooted in rebellion. The gospel does not erase creation; it restores what sin has damaged.

Male and Female: Equality of Worth and Complementarity of Design

One Humanity With Shared Dignity

Genesis 1:27 is explicit: "male and female He created them." Both are fully human. Both bear God's image. Both share the mandate to fill the earth and subdue it. Any attempt to treat women as less than human, less than morally significant, or less worthy of protection is a direct assault on the Creator's design.

At the same time, Genesis 2 emphasizes ordered complementarity. The woman is created as a suitable helper—language that does not imply inferiority, since Scripture can use "helper" of God Himself. The point is suitability and partnership. The man and woman are designed to work together, not compete for dominance. When sin enters, this harmony is strained, and the relationship becomes a common arena where selfishness and control show themselves. That distortion does not cancel the original design; it highlights what is broken and what redemption aims to heal.

Marriage and Family as the First Human Society

Genesis describes marriage as a covenantal bond: "a man will leave his father and his mother and will cling to his wife, and they will become one flesh." This is not presented as a late cultural invention but as a creational ordinance. It establishes a moral framework for sexuality, childrearing, and community stability. The Bible's later ethical teaching on faithfulness, adultery, divorce, and parental responsibility rests on this creation foundation.

The image of God is therefore not an abstract doctrine. It is lived out in homes, work, worship, and relationships. It shapes how people treat spouses, children, the vulnerable, and even enemies.

The Unity of the Human Person: Body, Breath, and Life

Man Is a Soul, Not a Soul Inside a Body

Genesis 2:7 says the man "became a living soul." In the Hebrew idiom, a "soul" is a living creature—a person. Man does not possess a soul as an immortal passenger; man is a soul as a unified living being. This fits the wider biblical pattern where "soul" can refer to the whole person, to life itself, or to a living creature. The language is flexible, but it does not teach natural immortality.

This matters for apologetics because many spiritual systems assume that what makes a person "really human" is an immortal inner essence. Scripture instead locates human identity in the whole person as God created him: embodied, living, responsible, and dependent. Eternal life is not a default human possession; it is a gift God grants through resurrection and continued life under His rule.

Death as the Cessation of Life, Not the Release of Consciousness

The warning in Genesis is straightforward: disobedience leads to death. Death is not described as a promotion into another conscious plane. It is the loss of life. Later Scripture consistently describes death as sleep, silence, and return to dust. The hope offered is not the survival of an immortal self but resurrection—God restoring life to the person who has died. That is why the New Testament repeatedly centers Christian hope on resurrection and the return of Christ.

The image of God, then, does not depend on an immortal soul. It depends on God's creative act and God's purpose for mankind. Even when life ends, God retains the ability to restore life, judge righteously, and grant everlasting life according to His standards.

Humanity's Commission: Work, Stewardship, and Worship

Cultivating the Earth Under Jehovah's Authority

Work is part of original human perfection. Genesis places Adam in the garden "to cultivate it and to take care of it." Labor is not a punishment; painful toil is. Productive work, creativity, and stewardship are part of mankind's designed dignity. This refutes the notion that spirituality requires escape from the material world. God made the physical world "good" and assigned humans to develop it responsibly.

Dominion also implies accountability. Humans do not own the earth in an absolute sense; they manage it under God. This principle shapes ethical decisions about honesty, business, property, justice, and compassion. When humans treat people as disposable or treat creation as meaningless, they contradict their role as image-bearers.

Worship as the Highest Human Purpose

Genesis assumes that human life is fundamentally God-directed. The command, the sanctuary-like garden setting, and the relational language all point to worshipful obedience. True human flourishing is not merely economic or emotional; it is moral and spiritual, rooted in right relationship with Jehovah.

For Christians, this worship is guided through the Spirit-inspired Word, not through mystical impressions or claims of inner spiritual voices. God's guidance comes through Scripture's clear teaching, applied with humility, prayer, and obedience.

The Image of God After the Fall

Defaced but Not Erased

Sin damages human moral life and distorts human thinking, but it does not erase the created reality of being made in God's image. This is why Scripture can command love for neighbor, justice for the oppressed, and protection for the innocent even in a fallen world. The image remains the basis for human rights and responsibilities.

At the same time, the New Testament speaks of renewal into Christlikeness. Jesus is the perfect image of God in human life—fully obedient, fully truthful, fully loving. Christians are called to imitate Him, not by allegorical imagination but by concrete obedience to His teaching. The restoration of the image is therefore ethical and relational: renewed knowledge of God, renewed righteousness, renewed love.

Implications for Human Value and Christian Witness

A biblical doctrine of mankind's creation refuses both despair and pride. It refuses despair because human life has real dignity by God's design. It refuses pride because humans are accountable creatures, dependent on God for life and breath. The image of God humbles arrogance and condemns cruelty. It also motivates evangelism, because people are not meaningless accidents; they are accountable image-bearers who need reconciliation with God through Christ.

Edward D. Andrews

CHAPTER 2 The Fall of Man: From Perfection to Imperfection in Eden

The Setting of Eden and the Reality of Original Uprightness

Genesis portrays the first humans as created good, placed in a prepared environment, and given meaningful work and moral instruction. The garden is not described as a mythic symbol but as a real place where real people lived under Jehovah's moral government. The command regarding the tree of the knowledge of good and bad establishes that Adam and Eve were not autonomous. They were free within boundaries, and those boundaries defined what obedience looked like.

The prohibition is not arbitrary. It is a test of loyalty expressed through a simple command. Humans were created to worship Jehovah through obedience. The tree becomes a clear line between trusting God's moral determination and seizing moral independence. The issue is not fruit. The issue is authority.

The Serpent's Deception and the Presence of Personal Evil

Satan's Strategy: Doubt, Distortion, and Denial

Genesis 3 introduces the serpent as crafty, and the broader testimony of Scripture identifies Satan as the real personal evil working behind the temptation. The serpent's approach is instructional for understanding how sin works: it begins by raising suspicion about God's goodness, then distorting God's words, and finally denying God's warning.

The serpent's question—"Did God really say...?"—targets the reliability and clarity of God's command. This is the first attack on the Word of God. It is not presented as intellectual curiosity. It is a calculated move to weaken trust. The serpent then shifts God's command into an exaggerated form, implying that God is restrictive and unreasonable. When Eve corrects the statement but adds her own fencing ("you must not touch it"), the conversation has already moved from obedient listening to negotiated reinterpretation. Finally, the serpent flatly denies the consequence: "You certainly will not die." That denial contradicts Jehovah directly and offers a new view of reality where God's warnings are not true.

The Lie About God and the Lie About Man

The serpent's promise, "you will be like God," reframes disobedience as advancement. This is the essence of temptation: treating rebellion as wisdom and autonomy as maturity. But the lie also includes a false anthropology. The serpent's denial of death implies that humans can rebel without real consequence. Scripture teaches the opposite: life is a gift, and sin ends in death.

This is not a minor doctrinal point. If death is not real death, the moral order collapses. God's warnings become empty, justice becomes unnecessary, and the cross becomes inexplicable. Genesis establishes from the beginning that God's moral government is real and that consequences are not negotiable.

The Act of Disobedience and Human Responsibility

Desire, Decision, and the Willingness to Transgress

Genesis describes Eve seeing that the tree was good for food, pleasing to the eyes, and desirable for gaining wisdom. The language shows the internal process: desire is stimulated, the mind rationalizes, and the will chooses. James later describes sin in similar terms: desire conceives and gives birth to sin, and sin results in death. Genesis is therefore not merely narrative; it is moral explanation.

Adam's participation is decisive. Scripture places primary responsibility on Adam, not because Eve is less accountable, but because Adam was given the command directly and functioned as head of the human family. His silence, his failure to guard, and his decision to eat represent a collapse of leadership under God. The fall is not an accident; it is willful disobedience.

Sin as Lawlessness, Not Mere Mistake

The New Testament defines sin as lawlessness. Genesis shows this in narrative form: God spoke; humans disobeyed. The fall is not portrayed as the result of ignorance but of transgression. They were not forced. They were deceived and enticed, but they chose. This matters because Scripture's call to repentance is always grounded in moral responsibility.

Immediate Consequences: Shame, Fear, and Broken Fellowship

The first result is not enlightenment but shame. Adam and Eve recognize their nakedness and attempt to cover themselves. Their covering is symbolic of a deeper reality: they sense exposure before God. Shame is the psychological echo of moral guilt. They then hide from Jehovah, which displays a new fear-driven posture toward the One who created them for fellowship.

Jehovah's questions in Genesis 3 are not requests for information. They are judicial and relational. God draws the offenders into confession. Yet both respond with blame-shifting. Adam points to Eve and, implicitly, to God ("the woman whom You gave"). Eve points to the serpent. The pattern of sin emerges immediately: disobedience, then concealment, then self-justification.

The Sentence of Death and the Loss of Access to Life

"Dust You Are": Death as Return to Nonlife

Jehovah's sentence includes the declaration that man will return to the dust. This language does not describe a conscious transition to another realm; it describes the end of life. The breath of life returns to God in the sense that life is withdrawn, and the person ceases to live. The soul, as the living person, does not continue as a conscious immortal entity. Death is the enemy, and the biblical hope is resurrection.

Exile and the Tree of Life

Adam and Eve are expelled from Eden so they cannot eat from the tree of life and live forever in a sinful state. This is both judgment and mercy. It is judgment because disobedience removes them from the sanctuary of God's presence. It is mercy because eternal life in corruption would mean endless sin, endless pain, and endless alienation. Jehovah's purpose is not to preserve sin forever but to remove it through redemption.

The Spread of Imperfection Through the Human Family

Sin and Death Enter the Human Race

Romans 5 teaches that sin entered the world through one man, and death through sin, and thus death spread to all because all sinned. This passage holds together two truths: inherited imperfection and personal accountability. Adam's sin brought the human race into a condition of corruption—mortality, weakness, disordered desire, and alienation. Yet each person also sins personally, confirming that the problem is not only inherited but also chosen.

This view avoids two errors. It avoids pretending that humans are born morally neutral and only become sinners by imitation. It also avoids fatalism that treats humans as incapable of meaningful moral response. Scripture holds both realities: humans are born into imperfection, and humans are responsible for their own sins.

The Early Evidence in Genesis 4–6

Genesis immediately shows the spread of sin in Cain's murder of Abel, in escalating violence, and in widespread wickedness. The narrative's speed is itself a theological point: once the relationship with God is severed, corruption grows quickly. Humanity becomes increasingly self-directed, and the earth becomes filled with violence. These are not merely ancient events; they reveal what human life becomes when it is detached from Jehovah's rule.

Jehovah's First Promise and the Necessity of Redemption

Genesis 3:15 introduces enmity between the serpent and the woman, between his seed and her seed, culminating in a decisive blow. Read historically and grammatically, this is a promise that evil will not triumph forever and that a deliverer will come. Scripture later identifies this deliverer in Jesus Christ, who came to give His life as a ransom and to destroy the works of the Devil.

The fall therefore sets the stage for the entire Bible's redemptive message. Humans need rescue not merely from bad habits but from condemnation, corruption, and death. God's answer is not to excuse sin but to address it through atonement and resurrection. The gospel is not God lowering His standards; it is God providing the means for sinners to be forgiven and for life to be restored.

CHAPTER 3 Exploring the Depth of Human Sinfulness: Heart, Mind, and Will Under Corruption

Sin Defined with Biblical Precision

Scripture does not treat sin as a vague label for human weakness. It defines sin in moral categories tied to God's law, God's character, and God's authority. First John states that sin is lawlessness. Paul describes sin as falling short of God's glory. Scripture also speaks of transgression, rebellion, impurity, deceit, and idolatry. These terms overlap, but they share one core meaning: sin is the creature refusing to live under the Creator's righteous rule.

This definition prevents two distortions. One distortion is minimizing sin as merely personal imperfection without guilt. The other distortion is redefining sin as merely social failure without reference to God. Biblical sin is always God-centered: it violates God's holiness and harms God's creatures.

The Condition of the Human Heart After Eden

Inner Corruption and Disordered Desire

After the fall, sin is not only an external behavior problem. Scripture repeatedly locates the root of sin in the heart. The heart in biblical usage refers to the inner person—thinking, desiring, valuing, choosing. Jesus teaches that out of the heart come evil thoughts and immoral actions. Jeremiah describes the heart as deceitful. These statements do not mean that every human acts as wickedly as possible, but they do mean that the inner human center is compromised.

Disordered desire is one of the clearest evidences of corruption. Humans routinely want what God forbids and resist what God commands. Pride seeks self-exaltation. Envy resents another's good. Lust reduces people to objects. Greed hoards rather than shares. These desires are not harmless impulses; they are moral dispositions that produce actions and shape identity.

Conscience and Accountability Remain

Even in corruption, humans retain conscience. Romans speaks of the work of the law written on hearts, with conscience bearing witness. Conscience can be ignored, dulled, or misinformed, but it continues to function as an inner testimony that humans are moral beings. This is part of why guilt is universal. People may deny God verbally, but they cannot erase the moral reality that their lives are accountable.

Because humans remain accountable, Scripture calls them to repent, believe, and obey. The call is not presented as theater. It is a summons that treats the listener as a responsible person. That is why evangelism matters. The gospel is not merely information; it is an appeal that demands response.

The Reach of Sin Without Denying Human Responsibility

Pervasive Corruption Without Fatalism

Scripture teaches that sin affects every area of human life: thought, desire, speech, behavior, relationships, and worship. Paul's indictment in Romans 1–3 is comprehensive, showing both outward acts and inward motivations. Yet Scripture does not teach that humans are mere machines. God's commands, warnings, and invitations assume meaningful moral agency.

A balanced biblical view recognizes that humans are born into imperfection and are inclined toward sin, while also recognizing that humans make real choices for which they are judged. This is why the New Testament can command believers to "put away" sinful practices and to "put on" righteous ones. Change is possible because God provides truth, discipline, community, and the power of the gospel.

The Role of Satan, Demons, and the World

Human sinfulness is intensified by external spiritual and cultural pressures. Scripture teaches that Satan deceives and that demons oppose God's purposes. The "world" in Johannine language often refers to the human system organized in rebellion against God. This means sin is not only personal; it is also promoted, normalized, and rewarded by structures that resist Jehovah's standards.

This perspective avoids blaming God for evil. The biblical narrative attributes moral evil to rebellious creatures—human and angelic. Human weakness and ignorance contribute to wrongdoing, but Scripture also speaks plainly of malicious spiritual influence and the seductive power of a corrupt world order.

Sin in Thought, Word, and Deed

Internal Sins That God Judges

Scripture does not limit sin to actions. Jesus condemns lustful looking and hateful contempt because they are moral failures in the inner person. Pride is condemned as a rival religion of the self. Unbelief is condemned because it treats God as untrustworthy. These are not minor matters. They reveal whether a person is submitting to God's truth or resisting it.

Because sin includes inward realities, repentance must also be inward. True repentance is not merely behavior management. It is a turning of the heart and mind—renouncing self-rule and returning to Jehovah's moral authority. This is why confession is essential. Confession is not informing God of what He does not know; it is agreeing with God's judgment about sin.

Speech as a Moral Barometer

Scripture treats the tongue as a powerful instrument for both good and evil. Lies, slander, harshness, manipulation, and corrupt speech are not social accidents; they are moral acts. Words reveal the heart's contents. A person who blesses God but curses people made in His likeness displays a contradiction that Scripture condemns.

Speech also affects community. Many sins become communal through words: false accusations, gossip, division, and hatred. The Bible's emphasis on truthfulness is therefore both theological and practical. Jehovah is a God of truth, and His people must reflect His character.

Actions That Reveal Worship

Sin is ultimately religious because it reflects what a person worships. Idolatry is not limited to statues. It includes trusting wealth, power, pleasure, or identity more than God. When Paul describes pagan moral collapse in Romans 1, he roots it in exchanging God's truth for a lie and worshiping created things. Wrong worship leads to wrong living.

This is why evangelism cannot be reduced to moral advice. The fundamental problem is not that people need better habits; it is that they need reconciliation with God through Christ.

The Universal Need for Redemption in Christ

The New Testament's diagnosis is universal: "all have sinned." This universality does not flatten differences between sins, nor does it deny that some lives show greater restraint than others. It means that no one can stand before God on the basis of personal righteousness. The standard is God's holiness, not comparative human goodness.

Jesus' sacrifice addresses sin at its root: guilt before God. His death is not merely an inspiring example. It is an atoning sacrifice that satisfies justice and opens the way for forgiveness. His resurrection confirms that death can be undone and that God's saving purpose is real.

Repentance, Faith, and the Path of Salvation

Salvation is presented in Scripture as a lived path: hearing the gospel, believing in Christ, repenting of sin, being baptized by immersion, and walking in obedience as a disciple. This is not salvation by human merit. It is salvation by God's grace received through faith that obeys. Faith that refuses obedience is not biblical faith; it is mere assent.

God guides His people through the Spirit-inspired Word. Christians are not instructed to seek inner voices or mystical impressions as authoritative guidance. They are instructed to learn, obey, and endure in faith, using Scripture as the standard for truth, correction, and training in righteousness.

Growth in Holiness as the Opposite of Sinfulness

Sinfulness is deep, but it is not unbeatable. Scripture calls Christians "holy ones" because they are set apart for God. This holiness is not a claim of sinless perfection; it is a calling to live differently. The Christian life includes confession, correction, discipline, and growth. When believers fail, they do not excuse sin; they repent and return to obedience.

The depth of sinfulness is therefore not a reason for despair. It is a reason to cling to Christ, submit to the Word, and cultivate habits of righteousness. The same Bible that exposes sin also provides the means for transformation through truth, community, and hope anchored in resurrection.

HUMAN IMPERFECTION

CHAPTER 4 The Nature and Consequences of Sin: Death, Corruption, and Divine Justice

The Nature of Sin Against Jehovah

Sin is not merely breaking an impersonal rule; it is personal rebellion against the Creator. Every sin says something about God in practice, even if not in words. It treats Him as less worthy of trust, less worthy of obedience, or less worthy of worship. Because God is holy, sin is fundamentally incompatible with fellowship with Him.

Sin also carries a relational dimension toward other humans. Since people are made in God's image, mistreating people is not only harm against them; it is contempt for the One whose likeness they bear. This is why Scripture links love for God with love for neighbor. You cannot claim to honor God while dishonoring those made by Him.

The Wages of Sin: Death

Death in Scripture as the End of Life

Romans states plainly: "the wages of sin is death." In biblical usage, death is not described as life in another form. It is the loss of life. The dead are not pictured as active participants in earthly affairs; they are in Sheol or Hades, the realm of the grave—gravedom. The consistent hope is resurrection, not the natural survival of an immortal soul.

This clarifies divine justice. If death is real death, then sin's seriousness is clear and the need for Christ's resurrection is central. If death is not real death, resurrection becomes a decorative idea rather than God's decisive answer to humanity's greatest enemy.

Gehenna as Eternal Destruction

Scripture also speaks of a final punishment beyond the grave. Gehenna is presented not as perpetual conscious torment but as final destruction—the irreversible end of life for the unrepentant. This aligns with the Bible's repeated contrast: eternal life versus destruction, life versus death. Eternal life is God's gift, not man's natural possession. Final judgment therefore results either in life granted or life forfeited.

Present Consequences of Sin in Human Life

Sin produces immediate effects even before final judgment. Guilt, shame, fear, and relational fracture are common. The conscience reacts because humans are moral creatures. Some attempt to silence conscience through denial, distractions, or hardened habits, but the moral reality remains. This is why people often feel both drawn to sin and haunted by it.

Sin also disorders society. When truth is abandoned, trust collapses. When sexual immorality spreads, families fracture. When greed rules, exploitation becomes normal. When violence is celebrated, the weak become prey. Scripture's descriptions of moral collapse are not exaggerations; they are sober observations about what happens when humans reject Jehovah's standards.

A fallen world also includes spiritual hostility. Satan and demons promote deception, division, and temptation. This does not remove human responsibility, but it explains why sin can feel both attractive and oppressive. The world system often rewards wrongdoing and mocks righteousness, creating constant pressure to compromise.

Sin Under Divine Justice: Judgment and Accountability

Jehovah's justice means He will judge sin. Scripture repeatedly affirms judgment according to deeds, with God's knowledge extending to motives and secrets. This is necessary for moral order. A universe without judgment would declare that evil and good are ultimately equal.

Divine judgment is not arbitrary. God's standards are revealed, and humans are judged as responsible creatures. This is why the gospel includes both warning and invitation. God does not merely announce condemnation; He offers forgiveness through Christ.

The Necessity of Atonement Through Christ's Sacrifice

Sin creates real guilt, and guilt requires real satisfaction of justice. The New Testament presents Jesus' death as an atoning sacrifice and a ransom. He gave His life for many. This language communicates substitution and deliverance: Christ takes the penalty that sinners deserve so that God can remain just while forgiving those who repent and believe.

Forgiveness is not God pretending sin does not matter. It is God dealing with sin at the cost of His Son's life. This also preserves the seriousness of moral law. God's mercy does not cancel His holiness; it honors it.

Forgiveness, Cleansing, and Ongoing Moral Transformation

Forgiveness addresses guilt before God, but sin's damage also includes habits, patterns, and relational fallout. Scripture therefore calls Christians to confession, cleansing, and renewed obedience. First John teaches that if we confess our sins, God is faithful and righteous to forgive and cleanse. Confession is not a ritual formula. It is an honest turning that rejects self-justification and submits to God's judgment.

The church's moral life also matters. Christians are called to holiness, to truth, and to love. Discipline and correction have a place, not as harsh control but as protection of the congregation's purity and the sinner's restoration. A church that excuses sin ceases to function as a light in a dark world.

Sin's Final Removal in God's Kingdom

Resurrection as Re-Creation and the Defeat of Death

The ultimate answer to sin's consequence is resurrection. God restores life to the person who has died. This is not the reawakening of an immortal part; it is the re-creation of the person by God's power. Jesus' resurrection is the guarantee that God can and will undo death. The Christian hope is therefore concrete: life restored, justice executed, righteousness established.

Christ's Return and the Thousand-Year Reign

Scripture presents Christ returning before the thousand-year reign. That reign is not an abstract symbol of human progress; it is God's appointed period in which Christ rules and the effects of sin are rolled back under His authority. The final goal is not an escape from earth but the restoration of life under God's rule, with the righteous enjoying everlasting life as God intended from the beginning.

This future hope motivates holiness now. A person who believes God will judge sin and reward righteousness cannot treat sin lightly.

Hope is not passive optimism; it is moral fuel for perseverance and obedience.

The Practical Consequences of Taking Sin Seriously

Taking sin seriously means refusing both despair and indulgence. Despair says sin is too deep for forgiveness. Indulgence says sin is too small to matter. The gospel rejects both. It declares that sin is serious enough to require Christ's death and that mercy is strong enough to forgive and transform the repentant.

This shapes daily life. Christians must pursue truthfulness, purity, humility, and love, not as self-improvement projects but as a response to God's mercy. Evangelism also becomes urgent, because sin has real consequences and Christ is the only Savior. The call is not to moralism but to repentance and faith expressed in obedient discipleship.

CHAPTER 5 Why Suffering Exists in God's Creation: Jehovah's Answer to Eden and Job

Jehovah's Original Purpose and the Moral Structure of Creation

Jehovah created humans to live as dependent moral agents under His righteous sovereignty, not as autonomous beings defining good and bad by personal preference. The opening chapters of Genesis present a world ordered by Jehovah's word, where life flourishes when humans accept His moral boundaries. That arrangement was not restrictive; it was protective. It grounded human freedom in truth, so choices would be made in harmony with the Creator's design.

Suffering, therefore, is not an "original feature" of Jehovah's creation. It enters the human experience when intelligent creatures—first spirit persons, then humans—reject Jehovah's rightful authority and choose a path that can only produce disorder, guilt, conflict, decay, and death. Scripture treats moral order as objective, not negotiable. When the moral Governor is rejected, the result is not liberation but collapse.

The Rebellion in Eden and the Abuse of Free Will

Genesis 3 records a deliberate challenge to Jehovah's sovereignty. The serpent's claim was not merely that humans could enjoy a different lifestyle, but that Jehovah's rulership was untrustworthy

HUMAN IMPERFECTION

and that humans would do better by determining morality for themselves. The temptation focused on independence: defining "good and bad" apart from Jehovah. Adam and Eve's sin was not an innocent mistake; it was a willful rejection of divine authority and a misuse of free will.

That rebellion introduced alienation: from Jehovah, from each other, and within the self. Shame appears immediately. Fear replaces peace. Blame replaces responsibility. Those are not arbitrary punishments imposed externally; they are the inward fruits of sin. When humans detach from the Source of life and moral clarity, suffering follows as a moral consequence, not as a defect in Jehovah's character.

The Satanic Accusation and the Issue of Sovereignty

The biblical narrative frames human suffering within a larger controversy involving Satan and other rebellious angels. Satan's challenge functions as an accusation: that Jehovah's way of ruling is not best, that His moral standards are oppressive, and that creatures would thrive more fully without Him. This is why Scripture repeatedly presents Jehovah as allowing a period in which human self-rule runs its course under the influence of demonic hostility, exposing the real outcomes of independence from God.

Jehovah's allowance is not moral weakness. It is moral clarity. The issue raised in Eden cannot be answered by raw force without leaving the deeper questions unresolved in the minds of moral creatures. If Jehovah simply eliminated rebels immediately, the accusation could be reframed as coercion. By allowing time, Jehovah demonstrates, in history and lived reality, what sin produces and what His righteousness preserves.

Why Jehovah Permits Inherited Sin and Human Brokenness

One of the hardest features of suffering is that it is inherited. Scripture teaches that Adam's sin introduced condemnation and death to his descendants. Paul explains: "Through one man sin entered into the world, and death through sin, and so death spread to all men." (Romans 5:12) This inherited condition means humans do not start from moral neutrality. We are born into weakness, disordered desires, and a world already bent away from Jehovah.

Jehovah's allowance of inherited sin serves the object lesson embedded in Eden: humans were not designed to live apart from God.

Human history confirms this with relentless consistency. When societies exalt autonomy, they do not become morally enlightened; they become fractured. When humans enthrone self, they do not find peace; they find rivalry. Inherited sin ensures the lesson is not theoretical. It presses into every generation that independence from Jehovah produces death, not freedom.

This does not make Jehovah the author of evil. Sin originates in creaturely rebellion. Jehovah's role is judicial permission within a bounded timeframe, directed toward a decisive resolution. Scripture never portrays Jehovah as delighting in human pain. It portrays Him as patient, purposeful, and committed to ending evil without compromising righteousness.

Job and the Question of Integrity Under Pressure

The account of Job reveals another layer of Satan's accusation: that humans serve Jehovah only when life is comfortable. Satan challenges Job's integrity, claiming devotion is merely transactional. The narrative exposes Satan as a slanderer and shows that faithfulness is possible even when circumstances become severe.

Job's experience also corrects a shallow view that every hardship is a direct punishment for a specific sin. Job's companions insisted suffering always indicates personal guilt. Jehovah rebuked their distorted reasoning. The point is not that Job understood every detail, but that Jehovah's righteousness stands, Satan's accusations fail, and human integrity is meaningful. Job's story places suffering within a moral arena where loyalty to Jehovah is real, chosen, and valuable.

Human Wickedness, Demonic Influence, and the Present World Order

Much suffering is plainly produced by human sin: violence, exploitation, deceit, sexual immorality, greed, addiction, neglect, and oppression. Scripture also teaches that demonic forces promote deception and hostility toward Jehovah's people. This does not remove human responsibility; it explains why evil often feels organized, persuasive, and spiritually corrosive.

The world's systems train people to call evil good and good evil, to normalize corruption, and to mock purity. When Scripture speaks of the "world," it refers not to the physical planet but to the human order arranged in opposition to Jehovah's standards. In such an environment, suffering increases because sin is multiplied and justified.

Natural Suffering and the Groaning of Creation

Not all suffering is directly inflicted by human hands. Disease, decay, disasters, and bodily weakness are woven into life in a fallen world. Scripture connects this to human sin and the resulting curse of death, not to a flaw in Jehovah's original design. The body was not made for endless decline. Death is an enemy. The creation "groans," reflecting the disharmony introduced by rebellion.

This is why the biblical hope is not escape into a disembodied existence, but resurrection—Jehovah restoring life by re-creating the person. Humans are not immortal souls trapped in bodies; humans are living souls, and death is the cessation of personhood. Jehovah's answer is not sentimental survival; it is the concrete act of raising the dead and restoring the earth to righteous life under Christ's Kingdom.

Jehovah's Righteous Permission and His Compassionate Help

Jehovah's allowance does not mean He is distant. Scripture consistently presents Him as near to the crushed in spirit and attentive to prayer. Yet His help operates within His purpose. He does not grant rebels the right to define reality while also shielding them from every consequence of rebellion. That would erase the object lesson. He does, however, provide guidance, comfort, restraint of evil, and a way of salvation through the ransom sacrifice of Jesus Christ.

Jesus' suffering and death are central. The cross is not a philosophical explanation; it is Jehovah's moral action in history. Sin is truly evil, death is truly horrific, and love is truly costly. Jehovah's solution is not to pretend evil is harmless, but to defeat it righteously through Christ's sacrifice and resurrection.

The Final Removal of Suffering and the Vindication of Jehovah's Name

The biblical trajectory moves toward a world where evil is removed, not managed. Satan and demons do not win an eternal stalemate; they face destruction. The wicked do not suffer forever; they face final removal. "Gehenna" represents irreversible destruction, not perpetual torment. The righteous do not float as immortal spirits; they inherit everlasting life as resurrected humans in a restored earth under Christ's Kingdom.

Jehovah's Name is vindicated when the truth becomes undeniable: His sovereignty is righteous, His moral standards protect life, and rebellion produces only misery and death. The present permission is temporary, purposeful, and bounded. It answers Eden. It answers the accusations showcased in Job. It demonstrates to all moral creatures that Jehovah's way is the only way that sustains life, peace, and holiness.

CHAPTER 6 Regaining Control: The Mind of Christ and Biblical Thinking

The Battle for the Mind and the Need for Biblical Control

Scripture treats the mind as the command center of the human life. What a person believes shapes what a person loves, chooses, and becomes. Sin distorts thinking, not only behavior. The fallen human condition includes rationalization, self-deception, and desires that pressure the will. In a world influenced by demonic deception and cultural corruption, minds drift unless they are actively trained by truth.

"Regaining control" is not self-salvation through willpower. It is the deliberate submission of the whole inner life to Jehovah through the Spirit-inspired Word. The aim is not merely external compliance but inner transformation, so that reactions, instincts, and habits increasingly reflect Christ.

The Meaning of Epignosis and Why Accurate Knowledge Changes a Person

The New Testament uses the term epignōsis to emphasize accurate, full, and penetrating knowledge. This is not trivia. It is truth grasped clearly enough to reshape conscience and conduct. When Christians take in accurate knowledge of Scripture and understand it in context, their thinking becomes anchored to reality rather than emotion, impulse, or social pressure.

Accurate knowledge trains moral perception. It strengthens discernment, so a person recognizes not only obvious sins but also subtle distortions: compromised motives, dishonest justifications, and hidden pride. Epignōsis creates stability because it ties the mind to Jehovah's revealed standards rather than shifting feelings.

Having the Mind of Christ in Its Biblical Sense

Paul writes: "We have the mind of Christ." (1 Corinthians 2:16) This does not mean mystical intuition or a private inner voice. It means believers have access to Christ's perspective through the inspired Scriptures that reveal His teaching, His priorities, and His pattern of obedience. To have the mind of Christ is to think in categories shaped by His words: love of truth, hatred of hypocrisy, compassion rooted in holiness, courage in obedience, and confidence in Jehovah's promises.

Philippians commands: "Have this mind among yourselves, which is yours in Christ Jesus." (Philippians 2:5) The context is humility and self-giving, not self-exaltation. The mind of Christ is a disciplined mindset that refuses self-worship and chooses obedience even when it costs.

Conscience Training and the Recalibration of Moral Reflexes

Conscience is not an infallible internal compass. It can be trained well or deformed. Scripture speaks of consciences that are weak, defiled, or seared. A believer regains control by retraining conscience through repeated exposure to Scripture, honest self-examination, and obedience in concrete decisions.

When conscience is trained biblically, it begins to function earlier and more accurately. Instead of warning only after sin has occurred, it warns when temptation first presents itself. It becomes sensitive to motives, not just actions. This is why biblical thinking must reach beyond "What is allowed?" to "What honors Jehovah?" and "What reflects Christ?"

Renewing the Mind Through the Word, Not Through Mystical Inner Guidance

Romans commands: "Be transformed by the renewal of your mind." (Romans 12:2) Renewal happens through Scripture understood and applied. The Holy Spirit does not indwell Christians as a private source of new revelation or internal messages. His guidance comes through the Spirit-inspired Word as it is studied, believed, and obeyed.

This keeps the Christian life grounded. It protects believers from confusion, emotionalism, and spiritual counterfeit. It also makes growth measurable: increasing accuracy in doctrine, increasing consistency in obedience, increasing Christlike reactions under pressure, and increasing clarity in moral choices.

Capturing Thoughts and Replacing Mental Scripts

Paul describes spiritual warfare in the realm of thought: "We take every thought captive to obey Christ." (2 Corinthians 10:5) Many destructive behaviors begin as repeated thought patterns: fantasies of revenge, rehearsals of lust, constant suspicion, anxious catastrophizing, and bitter narratives about self and others. These mental scripts become automatic, shaping the subconscious flow of reaction.

Biblical thinking interrupts the script. It challenges lies with truth, replacing distorted narratives with Jehovah's perspective. The Christian learns to ask: Is this thought true? Is it righteous? Does it align with Scripture? Does it honor Christ? This practice steadily changes what feels "natural." Over time, obedience becomes less forced because the inner narrative has changed.

The Heart, the Mind, and the Formation of Habitual Obedience

Scripture often uses "heart" to refer to the inner person: desires, intentions, and decisions. The mind supplies categories and judgments; the heart supplies affections and commitments. Regaining control requires both instruction and affection. Knowledge without love becomes cold. Love without knowledge becomes blind.

As Scripture reshapes both mind and heart, obedience becomes habitual. The believer's default responses begin to shift. Instead of immediate retaliation, there is patience. Instead of indulgence, there is self-control. Instead of panic, there is prayer and clear thinking. This is not perfectionism; it is maturation. Growth is seen in trajectories: fewer compromises, quicker repentance, deeper honesty, and stronger resolve to honor Jehovah.

The Role of Meditation, Memory, and Ongoing Correction

Biblical meditation is sustained reflection on Scripture so that truth sinks into the inner life. It is not emptying the mind; it is filling the mind with Jehovah's Word. Memory strengthens meditation because remembered Scripture can confront temptation in real time, including moments when a Bible is not open.

Correction remains essential because growth exposes new layers of sin and new areas requiring alignment. Christians regain control not by claiming they have arrived, but by submitting to continual refinement through Scripture. When the Word judges thoughts and intentions, it frees the believer from self-deception and trains a clear conscience.

Community, Shepherding, and the Practical Strengthening of the Mind

The New Testament assumes Christians grow in association with other believers. Teaching, encouragement, rebuke, and example are instruments Jehovah uses. Isolation weakens discernment; it magnifies private rationalizations. Godly association strengthens biblical thinking because it places one's life under shared accountability and shared truth.

Shepherding, when done biblically, does not replace personal responsibility. It supports it. The aim is to help believers apply Scripture accurately, identify blind spots, and pursue holiness with practical consistency.

CHAPTER 7 Foreknowledge: God's Insight into the Future and the Question of Molinism

Foreknowledge as a Biblical Attribute of Jehovah

Scripture presents Jehovah as the One who knows reality exhaustively and declares His purposes without uncertainty. He is not one being among many learning as events unfold; He is the Creator standing above time and history. Prophecy is one clear display: Jehovah announces what will happen and then brings it to pass, demonstrating that His knowledge is not guesswork.

At the same time, Scripture holds humans morally responsible as genuine decision-makers. Commands, warnings, promises, and judgments presuppose real accountability. The biblical framework therefore affirms both divine foreknowledge and meaningful human choice.

What Foreknowledge Is and What It Is Not

Foreknowledge is Jehovah's knowledge of future events before they occur. It is not the same thing as causation. Knowing that an event will happen does not force the event to happen. Scripture distinguishes between Jehovah's sovereign action—what He directly brings about—and human actions for which humans are accountable.

This distinction matters because many theological errors collapse knowledge into determinism. The Bible does not. It portrays Jehovah as able to accomplish His redemptive purposes while also holding individuals responsible for sins they freely choose.

The Biblical Data: Prophecy, Prediction, and Human Accountability

Scripture contains unconditional prophecies that Jehovah declares and fulfills, and conditional warnings where outcomes change based on human response. The conditional structure appears in many prophetic calls to repentance, where judgment is announced but mercy is offered if people turn from wickedness. This does not weaken Jehovah's foreknowledge; it demonstrates His sovereign freedom to set conditions and to respond consistently with His stated moral standards.

The New Testament also describes events surrounding Jesus' death as known in advance while simultaneously assigning guilt to those who carried it out. Acts speaks of Jesus being delivered up according to God's determined plan and foreknowledge, while also holding lawless men accountable for murdering Him. Divine foreknowledge and human guilt are placed together without apology because Scripture does not treat them as contradictions.

Molinism Defined in Plain Terms

Molinism is a philosophical model that attempts to explain how Jehovah can know future free decisions without causing them. It argues that God possesses not only knowledge of what will happen, but also knowledge of what any free creature would do in any set of circumstances. This is often called "middle knowledge," positioned logically between God's knowledge of all possibilities and His knowledge of what He will bring about.

In this model, Jehovah knows counterfactuals of creaturely freedom: statements such as, "If person X were in circumstance Y, that person would choose Z." On that basis, Jehovah can order history to accomplish His purposes while allowing genuinely free decisions.

Natural Knowledge, Middle Knowledge, and Free Knowledge

Molinism typically speaks of three logical aspects of divine knowledge. "Natural knowledge" refers to Jehovah's perfect grasp of all possibilities, including every way reality could be. "Middle knowledge" refers to His knowledge of how free creatures would act under particular conditions. "Free knowledge" refers to His knowledge of the actual history that will occur as He chooses to create and govern a particular world order.

This framework is an attempt to preserve both divine sovereignty and libertarian free will. It insists Jehovah does not learn, does not guess, and does not need to override freedom to accomplish His will. He achieves His purposes through His comprehensive knowledge and His wise governance.

Evaluating Molinism Under the Authority of Scripture

The key question is not whether Molinism is clever, but whether it stays within what Scripture affirms and refuses what Scripture denies. Scripture clearly teaches Jehovah's exhaustive knowledge and His ability to bring His purposes to completion. It also clearly teaches human responsibility and the reality of meaningful choices.

Molinism can be useful as an explanatory tool if it is treated as subordinate to Scripture and if it avoids turning Jehovah into a being constrained by "counterfactual truths" outside Himself. Jehovah is not a manager of external facts; He is the absolute Lord of reality. Any model that implies God is limited by a grid of truths independent of Him undermines His sovereignty.

A biblically faithful use of Molinism therefore insists that if Jehovah knows counterfactuals, He knows them because His knowledge is perfect and because His governance is perfect, not because He is beholden to an abstract realm of realities that dictate what He may do.

Foreknowledge and Freedom Without Fatalism

Many Christians struggle with a practical fear: if Jehovah knows my choice in advance, is my choice real? Scripture answers by treating human decisions as real and accountable even while Jehovah's foreknowledge remains perfect. The biblical writers do not speak as though people are acting out a script against their will. They call for repentance, warn of judgment, and praise obedience because choices are meaningful.

Foreknowledge does not remove deliberation. Humans still weigh reasons, pursue desires, resist pressure, and choose. Jehovah's knowledge is not a temporal observation waiting in the future; it is the Creator's comprehensive grasp of history. His knowing does not force the will. It simply means nothing surprises Him.

Judas, Peter, and the Difference Between Prediction and Coercion

Jesus foretold Peter's denial and spoke of betrayal. These predictions did not force those actions; they revealed Jesus' accurate knowledge and the moral weakness of human hearts under pressure. Peter was responsible, and Peter also repented. Judas was responsible, and Judas chose betrayal for corrupt reasons. The narrative does not treat them as puppets. It treats them as accountable men whose actions were foreknown.

This illustrates the biblical pattern: Jehovah can foreknow human sins without being the author of those sins. The moral blame belongs to the human agent. Foreknowledge is not moral participation.

Jehovah's Freedom to Reveal or Withhold Foreknowledge

Scripture presents Jehovah as revealing future events when it serves His purpose, not because He is obligated to disclose everything.

Prophecy is selective revelation, not the full disclosure of omniscience. This means Christians should not treat foreknowledge as a curiosity to be mined for speculation. The revealed purpose of foreknowledge is to strengthen faith, confirm Jehovah's sovereignty, and anchor obedience in hope.

The Practical Effect of Foreknowledge on Trust and Obedience

Foreknowledge grounds confidence. Evil is not winning. History is not drifting. Jehovah's Kingdom purpose does not depend on human cleverness. At the same time, foreknowledge intensifies responsibility. Since Jehovah knows hearts and outcomes, self-deception is futile. The proper response is not fatalism but humility, repentance, and disciplined obedience.

Jehovah's foreknowledge also reinforces the Christian hope of resurrection and restoration. Death is not the doorway to a conscious afterlife; it is the end of life until Jehovah restores the person by resurrection. The One who knows the end from the beginning is fully able to remember, restore, and re-create those who belong to Him.

CHAPTER 8 Navigating Life with Free Will: Freedom Under Jehovah's Sovereignty

Free Will Defined Biblically as Responsible Choice Within Real Limits

"Free will" in Scripture is not the fantasy of absolute autonomy. Humans are not independent gods. They are created persons with real agency who make meaningful choices within boundaries set by Jehovah's sovereignty, moral law, and the realities of a fallen world. Freedom is therefore relative, not absolute.

This biblical definition fits the texture of ordinary life. People choose, and those choices matter. Yet no one chooses their birth era, genetic weaknesses, early influences, or the fact of death. Even in those constraints, Scripture addresses humans as responsible, calling for repentance, faith, and obedience. The Bible never treats humans as machines. It treats them as accountable moral agents who can respond to Jehovah.

Jehovah's Sovereignty as the Foundation, Not the Rival, of Human Freedom

Jehovah's sovereignty is not a threat to freedom; it is what makes freedom meaningful. Without a moral Governor, "freedom" becomes the rule of appetite, power, and manipulation. Jehovah's sovereignty provides objective categories of good and bad, establishes justice, and offers guidance that protects life.

When Scripture calls Jehovah "King," it does not portray Him as insecure. It portrays Him as righteous. His authority is the authority of the Creator who knows what humans are and what leads to their flourishing. Human freedom is healthiest when it functions within Jehovah's design.

The Eden Pattern: Freedom With a Moral Boundary

In Eden, Adam and Eve had expansive freedom with a clear moral boundary: they were to trust Jehovah's definition of good and bad. The boundary was not arbitrary. It expressed a permanent truth: humans are not qualified to define morality independently of the Creator. When that boundary was rejected, freedom did not expand; it collapsed into shame, fear, alienation, and death.

This pattern repeats. When people insist on absolute autonomy, they do not become freer; they become enslaved—often to lust, pride, bitterness, and the approval of others. Scripture describes sin as slavery because it captures the will through disordered desire and false reasoning.

Inherited Sin and the Realistic Limits on Human Choice

Humans inherit sin and death through Adam. This inherited condition does not erase choice, but it weakens it. It tilts desires toward selfishness and makes holiness costly. It also places humans in a world where temptation is constant and where demonic deception amplifies confusion.

This is why biblical instruction does not assume people can "just do better" by determination alone. It insists on truth, discipline, and dependence on Jehovah's guidance through Scripture. The Christian life is a path of renewed thinking and re-formed desires, not instant moral perfection.

Scripture's Calls to Choose and the Reality of Accountability

The Bible repeatedly places choices before humans: "Choose life," "turn," "repent," "do not harden your hearts," "flee immorality," "pursue righteousness." These commands presume the hearer can respond. Jehovah's justice would be incoherent if humans had no real agency.

At the same time, Scripture acknowledges that choices are influenced. People can be "enslaved to sin," "darkened in understanding," and "deceived." This means that navigating life with free will requires more than choice; it requires the formation of wisdom. The will must be educated by truth, or it will be steered by appetite and pressure.

Freedom in Christ: Liberation From Sin's Control, Not Freedom from Jehovah

Jesus does not free humans from Jehovah; He frees them for Jehovah. Christian freedom is deliverance from sin's mastery and from the fear-driven patterns of the world. It is the freedom to obey with a clean conscience and steady hope.

This freedom is not license. Scripture rejects the idea that grace is permission to indulge sin. Instead, grace equips believers to say no to ungodliness and yes to holiness. The Christian is not guided by impulses, omens, or inner voices, but by the Spirit-inspired Word that trains judgment and reshapes desire.

Wisdom as the Skill of Making Choices Under Pressure

Navigating life is rarely a matter of choosing between obvious good and obvious evil. More often it is choosing between good and better, between immediate relief and long-term faithfulness, between pleasing people and pleasing Jehovah. Wisdom is the skill of applying Scripture to complex life situations.

Wisdom includes understanding consequences. Sin promises immediate gratification while hiding future pain. Jehovah's commands often require restraint now for life later. Biblical wisdom therefore strengthens the will by strengthening vision: it teaches a person to value what Jehovah values and to measure choices by truth rather than impulse.

The Role of Prayer, Counsel, and Discipline in Strengthening the Will

Prayer aligns the heart with Jehovah's standards and brings hidden motives into the light. It does not replace decision-making; it purifies it. Godly counsel also strengthens freedom because it exposes blind spots and interrupts self-justification. Discipline—consistent habits of obedience—builds moral strength. Over time, what once felt impossible becomes practiced.

This is especially important because many choices are made quickly. In such moments, people do not rise to the level of their intentions; they act from their trained patterns. This is why Scripture commands believers to set their minds on what is true and righteous, to guard the heart, and to cultivate self-control.

The Hope That Stabilizes Choices: Resurrection and the Restoration of Life

Freedom is strengthened by hope. If life is only what can be grasped now, people will choose short-term pleasure and self-protection. Scripture offers a larger horizon: Jehovah will restore life through resurrection, and He will establish righteous life under Christ's Kingdom. Death is not a transition into conscious existence; it is the end of life until resurrection. That hope stabilizes decisions because it places present costs in the light of future restoration.

It also reframes suffering. A believer does not interpret hardship as proof Jehovah has abandoned them. Hardship exists in a world under sin and demonic hostility, but Jehovah's promises remain steady. The Christian chooses faithfulness not because it is always easy, but because it is true, and because Jehovah's Kingdom purpose will prevail.

Edward D. Andrews

CHAPTER 9 The Guidance of the Holy Spirit in Christian Life

The Holy Spirit's Work and the Christian's Daily Direction

Christian living requires real guidance, not vague impressions or inward voices. Jehovah has never left His people without clear direction, but His method is rooted in truth, not mysticism. The Holy Spirit guides Christians, yet not by literally dwelling inside believers as a personal resident. Rather, the Holy Spirit's guidance is exercised through the Spirit-inspired Word of God, which provides

HUMAN IMPERFECTION

the content, the standards, the correction, and the practical wisdom needed for faithfulness.

This approach protects Christians from spiritual instability. If "guidance" is treated as private inner messaging, then the authority shifts from Scripture to subjective feeling. One believer's "impression" conflicts with another's "leading," and both can be sincere while both are wrong. Jehovah does not shepherd His people with confusion. He provides a fixed revelation that can be read, tested, taught, and obeyed. The Holy Spirit is the divine Agent behind that revelation, and Christians are guided by submitting to what He has already given in Scripture.

Edward D. Andrews

The Spirit's Guidance Begins With Inspiration, Not Inner Occupation

The Spirit as the Divine Source of Scripture

The most foundational work of the Holy Spirit is the production of Scripture. The Bible does not present itself as a collection of religious reflections, but as God-breathed revelation. The Spirit moved the prophets and apostles so that what they wrote was what Jehovah wanted written, in the words He intended, communicated through their personalities and vocabulary without corrupting the message. This is why Scripture is not merely helpful; it is authoritative. It is the standard by which beliefs and conduct are measured.

When Christians say they are "guided by the Holy Spirit," the first and most concrete meaning is that they are guided by what the Spirit has revealed. The Spirit's guidance is therefore public, objective, and testable. It does not depend on a believer's temperament, emotional condition, or imagination. It depends on the written Word.

The Spirit's Guidance as the Sword, Not an Inner Whisper

The New Testament describes the Word of God as "the sword of the Spirit." A sword is not a vague sensation. It is an instrument with shape, edge, and purpose. The Spirit's sword cuts through deception, exposes motive, and defends against temptation. This metaphor makes the Spirit's guidance inseparable from Scripture. If a Christian neglects Scripture, he is not merely neglecting information; he is setting aside the Spirit's appointed means of direction.

What "Filled With the Spirit" Means in the Biblical Sense

The Parallel Between Being Filled and Letting the Word Dwell

Some assume that "being filled with the Spirit" must mean a literal indwelling. Yet Scripture itself provides a clarifying parallel. One passage calls believers to be filled with the Spirit; another calls believers to let the word of Christ dwell in them richly. The overlap in outcomes is striking: gratitude, worship, wise speech, and obedient living. The point is not that a divine Person takes up internal residence in a physical sense, but that the Christian is shaped, governed, and moved by the message the Spirit has given.

To be "filled," then, is to be directed. It is to be so saturated with Scriptural truth that it becomes the controlling influence in decisions, relationships, and priorities. The Spirit's influence is real, but it comes through the Word that He inspired and through the believer's obedient response to that Word.

The Spirit's Work in Conviction and Correction Through Scripture

Jehovah corrects His people by exposing sin, confronting rationalizations, and training righteousness. Scripture is explicitly said to accomplish these tasks so that the man of God may be fully equipped for every good work. Guidance is therefore not merely about "which option should I choose," but about "what kind of person must I become." The Spirit guides Christians into maturity by means of the biblical pattern of teaching, reproof, correction, and training.

Passages Often Used for Indwelling and Their Scriptural Sense

"The Spirit Dwells in You" as Covenant Belonging and Divine Ownership

The New Testament can speak of God's Spirit "in" believers as a way of describing divine ownership, covenant relationship, and the visible evidence of God's power at work among His people. Scripture often uses "in" language for influence and relationship, not for physical location. God's Word can be said to be "in" someone when it is internalized. Faith can be "in" the heart. Sin can "dwell" in someone in the sense that it exercises influence and produces behavior. The same semantic range applies when Scripture speaks of God's Spirit in relation to believers. The point is not a literal internal habitation, but the reality that Christians are identified as those who live under the Spirit's direction as revealed in the gospel and Scriptures.

The Temple Language and the Corporate People of God

Scripture also calls the congregation God's temple. In context, this language frequently emphasizes the corporate people of God as the sphere where Jehovah's presence is recognized, not the idea that each individual body becomes a mystical container for a resident Spirit. Jehovah's presence among His people is real and powerful, but it is expressed through worship, obedience, discipline, preaching, and the sanctifying effects of Scriptural truth.

How the Spirit Guides Christians in Practical Decision-Making

Wisdom, Not Omens: The Spirit-Given Pattern for Choices

Christians face decisions about work, marriage, parenting, friendships, ministry, and conscience matters not spelled out as direct commands. The Spirit guides through the wisdom framework of Scripture. That includes moral boundaries, priorities, and principles that shape judgment. A Christian does not need an inner voice to know he must be honest, sexually pure, peaceable, hardworking, and generous. Scripture already commands these things, and Scripture trains discernment so that believers can apply God's standards to complex situations.

This is why biblical wisdom literature remains vital. Proverbs trains patterns of thinking. Psalms trains worship and emotional order under Jehovah. The Gospels train imitation of Christ. The letters train congregational health, self-control, doctrinal clarity, and endurance. The Spirit guides by building a mind that thinks God's thoughts after Him, in the sense that the believer increasingly reasons according to Scripture.

Prayer and Guidance Without Mystical Indwelling

Prayer is essential, but prayer is not a device for receiving secret information. Prayer is fellowship with Jehovah through Christ, expressing dependence, confession, gratitude, requests, and submission. Jehovah answers prayer according to His will, and the Christian learns His will through Scripture. Prayer therefore works hand in hand with Bible study. A believer prays for wisdom, then searches Scripture, then applies Scriptural principles with a trained conscience, seeking counsel from mature Christians who likewise submit to the Word.

Counsel, Congregation, and the Spirit's Orderly Means

Jehovah uses the congregation for instruction and protection. The Spirit-inspired Word provides qualifications for overseers and shepherds and sets the boundaries of teaching. When mature Christians counsel from Scripture, the guidance is not merely human opinion; it is an application of the Spirit's revealed truth. This preserves unity and guards the flock from private revelations that cannot be tested.

The Danger of Replacing Scripture With Subjective "Leadings"

The Problem of Competing Inner Messages

History and daily experience show that subjective "leadings" can justify almost anything: sinful relationships, reckless financial decisions, doctrinal novelty, prideful independence from the congregation, and spiritual elitism. Once a person equates his internal sense with divine guidance, correction becomes nearly impossible. Scripture, however, is designed to correct. It stands above all believers equally. It humbles the proud and steadies the unstable.

The Biblical Test of Teaching and Spirits

The New Testament commands believers to test teachings and spiritual claims. The standard for that test is apostolic truth—what has been delivered in Scripture. This assumes that false spiritual claims will arise and that the remedy is not better intuition but better adherence to the Word. The Spirit's guidance is therefore safest where it is most concrete: the Scriptures.

The Spirit's Guidance and Christian Growth in Holiness

Transformation Through Renewed Thinking

Christian growth is not fueled by mystical infusion but by renewed thinking and obedient action. Scripture reshapes desires, habits, and speech. It teaches the believer to put off the old personality and put on the new. The Spirit guides by means of truth embraced and practiced. As the believer submits to Scripture, he becomes more stable, more discerning, and more equipped for good works.

Endurance in a Wicked World with a Fixed Standard

Christians live in a world influenced by Satan and demons and shaped by human imperfection. Guidance must therefore be steady. Scripture provides that steadiness. It sets the Christian's hope, warns of deception, and calls for endurance. The believer is not left to interpret life by mood or trend. He is anchored to what Jehovah has spoken.

Edward D. Andrews

CHAPTER 10 God's Purpose for Humanity and Earth

Jehovah's Stated Purpose: An Inhabited, Cultivated Earth Under Human Stewardship

Jehovah's purpose for humanity and the earth is not hidden. It is plainly stated at creation and reaffirmed throughout Scripture. Humanity was made in God's image to represent His rule on earth by exercising righteous dominion, cultivating the world, building family life, and extending the order of Eden outward. The earth was not created as a temporary stage to be discarded. Scripture explicitly states that Jehovah formed the earth to be inhabited. That single truth shapes the whole biblical storyline: creation, human rebellion, redemption through Christ, resurrection hope, and the restoration of God's original purpose.

Genesis presents Jehovah's intent in simple terms. Humanity is commissioned to fill the earth and subdue it, not as exploiters, but as responsible stewards under Jehovah. Genesis also describes Eden as a place to be cultivated and guarded, showing that work, care, and purposeful labor were part of perfection, not a punishment. Later Scripture confirms that the righteous will possess the earth and live forever on it. The Bible's hope is not the abandonment of earth, but the triumph of Jehovah's righteousness on earth.

The Meaning of Being Made in God's Image

Representation Under God, Not Independence from God

To be made in God's image is to be designed for moral responsibility, rational thought, relational capacity, and delegated authority. It does not mean humans become divine. It means humans are to represent Jehovah's standards on earth. Authority was given, but it was never autonomous. Human dominion was meant to mirror God's own righteous rule: truthful, just, compassionate, orderly, and life-giving.

Genesis 1:26 presents the image and the commission together. The image is connected to the assignment: humanity is to exercise dominion over the animals and the earth. This dominion is not permission for cruelty. It is stewardship. The Creator cares for His creation; His image-bearers are to care for it in His ways.

Family, Culture, and the Expansion of Ordered Life

The command to be fruitful and multiply shows that family life is not a concession to imperfection but part of Jehovah's purpose. Humanity was to spread, develop, cultivate, and extend the blessings of God's order across the planet. This includes responsible use of resources, creative development, meaningful labor, and social life shaped by righteousness.

Genesis 2:15 and the Dignity of Work in God's Design

Cultivating and Guarding as a Perfect Calling

Genesis 2:15 states that Jehovah placed the man in the garden to cultivate it and to keep it. This reveals that work is dignified and purposeful. It is not presented as burdensome toil, but as meaningful activity aligned with creation. Cultivation implies development, planning, and care. Guarding implies protection, attentiveness, and responsibility.

This is critical for understanding the Bible's view of the future. The hope of paradise earth is not eternal idleness. It is life as Jehovah intended: productive, joyful, safe, and righteous. The earth was designed for human life under God, and Scripture never revokes that design.

The Moral Context of Guarding

The instruction to guard the garden also implies that human responsibility includes resisting what threatens righteousness. Later events show how vital this was. Human failure opened the door to sin and death. Yet Jehovah's purpose did not collapse. It was opposed by rebellion, but it was never cancelled.

Isaiah 45:18 and the Earth as a Permanent Home for Humanity

Formed to Be Inhabited

Isaiah 45:18 states that Jehovah created the earth not as a wasteland but formed it to be inhabited. This is a direct affirmation of purpose. The earth is not a disposable object. It is the intended home for human life. This passage also ties creation to God's righteousness and sovereignty. Jehovah's designs are not frustrated by human rebellion. His stated purpose stands.

This has direct implications for Christian hope. If Jehovah created the earth to be inhabited, then the biblical expectation is restoration, not escape. The future includes the removal of wickedness and the establishment of righteousness, not the abandonment of God's handiwork.

Harmony With the Broader Scriptural Witness

Throughout Scripture, the earth is portrayed as the arena where Jehovah's name will be vindicated and His standards will be honored. The repeated promise that the meek will inherit the earth and that the righteous will live forever upon it aligns with Isaiah 45:18. The continuity is clear: creation's purpose remains, redemption serves that purpose, and the final outcome is the earth filled with righteous inhabitants.

Psalm 37:29 and the Promise of Everlasting Life on Earth

The Righteous Will Possess the Earth

Psalm 37:29 states that the righteous will possess the earth and dwell forever on it. The wording is not temporary. It is enduring. This promise is not presented as a metaphor for heaven, but as a direct statement about the earth. The psalm contrasts the brief success of the wicked with the lasting inheritance of the righteous. Jehovah's justice is shown not merely by punishing evil, but by establishing a stable, permanent home for the faithful.

Meekness, Trust, and the Moral Shape of the Inheritance

Psalm 37 emphasizes trust in Jehovah, patience, and refusal to imitate the wicked. The inheritance of the earth is tied to character shaped by submission to Jehovah. This shows that God's purpose for the earth is inseparable from God's purpose for humans: a population that loves righteousness.

Psalm 98:6-8 and Creation's Joy Under Jehovah's Rule

The Earth Rejoices When Jehovah's Kingship Is Manifest

Psalm 98:6-8 depicts the earth responding with joy as Jehovah's kingship is celebrated and His righteous judgments are anticipated. The imagery of seas roaring and rivers clapping is poetic, but the theological point is direct: Jehovah's righteous rule brings blessing to the created order. The earth is not treated as a disposable backdrop. It is included in the vision of joy when divine righteousness is established.

This confirms that God's purpose includes the earth itself enjoying peace and order. When wickedness is removed, creation is no longer subjected to the corruption humans have introduced. Jehovah's judgments are not destructive of His purpose; they are restorative, clearing away what opposes righteousness.

The Entrance of Sin and Death Did Not Cancel Jehovah's Purpose

Human Imperfection and a Wicked World

Human rebellion introduced sin and death. Death is not a doorway to a higher life by nature; it is the cessation of personhood. Humans are souls, and when life ends, the person is gone until resurrection. This makes Jehovah's purpose for earth even more significant: He intends a righteous world where death is removed and life is secure under His standards.

Redemption Serves Restoration

Jehovah's response to human rebellion was not to abandon the earth but to provide redemption through Christ. The atonement answers guilt and opens the path to resurrection life. The future hope includes resurrected humans living in a righteous society on earth, fulfilling the original mandate in a perfected condition.

The Christian's Relationship to God's Purpose Today

Stewardship in the Present Reflects the Future

Christians honor Jehovah's purpose by living as faithful stewards now. That includes honest work, moral purity, love for neighbor, care for family, and refusal to live as if the present world's values are ultimate. Christian ethics are not detached from creation. They are aligned with Jehovah's design and anticipate the future when righteousness prevails.

Worship and Hope Rooted in Jehovah's Declared Intention

A Christian's hope is strengthened when he recognizes that God's purpose is stated plainly. Jehovah formed the earth to be inhabited. He made humans to cultivate and guard. He promised that the righteous will live forever on the earth. These truths anchor faith and protect believers from ideas that dismiss the earth as irrelevant.

CHAPTER 11 Christ's Sacrifice: The Ultimate Hope for Fallen Humanity

The Problem Christ Solves: Sin, Death, and Human Powerlessness

Humanity's greatest problem is not lack of information, education, or social improvement. The greatest problem is sin and the death it produces. Sin is rebellion against Jehovah's moral authority, expressed in both acts and the inward bent of fallen humans. Death is the consequence: not transformation into another conscious mode of existence, but the end of personhood. Humans are souls; they do not possess immortal souls. When a human dies, the person ceases. If there is hope beyond death, it must come from Jehovah's power to restore life by resurrection.

This is precisely what Christ's sacrifice addresses. The Bible presents Jesus' death as a ransom price, a substitutionary sacrifice that satisfies justice and opens the way for forgiveness and life. The atonement is not merely an example of love, though it is that. It is a legal and moral provision within Jehovah's righteous standards. Jehovah does not ignore sin; He deals with it. Christ's sacrifice is the God-provided solution that upholds justice while extending mercy.

The Biblical Meaning of Sacrifice and Ransom

The Ransom Concept and the Value of a Perfect Life

Scripture uses the language of "ransom" to explain Christ's death. A ransom is a price paid to release captives. Humanity is captive to sin and death. A perfect human life was lost through Adam's disobedience, bringing death to Adam's descendants. The ransom must correspond to what was lost: a perfect human life. Jesus, as a sinless man, offered His life in obedience to Jehovah, providing the corresponding price that justice requires.

This is not cold transaction; it is moral coherence. Jehovah's standards are consistent. Life is sacred. Sin brings death. Forgiveness must be grounded in righteousness. The ransom provides that foundation, enabling Jehovah to forgive repentant sinners without compromising His justice.

Substitution Without Confusion

Christ's sacrifice is substitutionary in the biblical sense. He died for others, in their place regarding the penalty of sin, so that they might live. This does not mean Jehovah punished an unwilling victim. Jesus willingly offered Himself in obedience and love. Jehovah lovingly gave His Son, and the Son lovingly gave Himself. The unity of Father and Son is expressed in aligned purpose, not in a denial of justice.

The Historical Reality of Christ's Death and Its Redemptive Meaning

The Execution of Jesus and the Fulfillment of Jehovah's Saving Plan

Jesus' execution occurred in 33 C.E. on Nisan 14. The timing matters because it anchors the atonement in real history, not myth. The Gospels present a public event under Roman authority, witnessed by disciples and enemies. The apostolic preaching depended on this historical core: Jesus was executed, buried, and raised. The sacrifice is not merely theological theory; it is a historical act with divine meaning.

The Cross as the Intersection of Justice and Mercy

At the cross, Jehovah's justice is displayed because sin is not dismissed. Jehovah's mercy is displayed because He provides the sacrifice Himself through His Son. The cross exposes the seriousness of sin and the depth of divine love. It also shows that salvation is not achieved by human effort. Fallen humans cannot undo sin's guilt or reverse death's power. Only Jehovah can provide the remedy, and He did so through Christ.

The Resurrection and the Defeat of Death

Death as Cessation and the Necessity of Resurrection

If death were a continuation of conscious life, resurrection would be reduced to a secondary feature. Scripture treats resurrection as essential because death is real, final, and destructive to human life. The hope for those who die is not their survival in another realm by nature. The hope is Jehovah's power to re-create the person. Resurrection is restoration of life by God's memory and power, returning the person to conscious existence.

Jesus' Resurrection as the Guarantee of Future Resurrection

Jesus' resurrection is the cornerstone of Christian hope. Jehovah raised Him, vindicating His righteousness and proving that death does not have ultimate authority. Because Jehovah raised Jesus, Christians can trust that Jehovah will raise others. Christ's sacrifice removes the legal barrier of sin, and His resurrection demonstrates the power that will bring the dead back to life.

Forgiveness and Moral Transformation Flow From the Atonement

Justification and Cleansed Conscience

Christ's sacrifice provides forgiveness for repentant sinners who exercise faith. This is not sentimental forgiveness. It is grounded in the ransom. A cleansed conscience means the believer is no longer crushed by guilt before Jehovah. He can approach God with confidence, not because he is perfect, but because Jehovah has accepted Christ's sacrifice as the basis for pardon.

Redemption Produces a New Way of Life

The atonement also demands transformation. Christ did not die to leave people in sin. He died to free them from sin's mastery. Those who receive forgiveness are called to live in holiness, turning away from immorality, dishonesty, violence, and the corrupt patterns of a wicked world. The sacrifice changes both status before God and direction of life. Faith that refuses obedience is not biblical faith.

The Universal Scope of Hope: Fallen Humanity and Jehovah's Open Invitation

The Offer of Life as a Gift

Eternal life is not a natural human possession. It is a gift. Humans do not have immortality by nature; they can receive everlasting life by Jehovah's grace through Christ. This removes boasting and centers gratitude. The Christian's hope rests in God's generosity and the completed work of Christ, not in personal merit.

The Call to Repentance, Faith, and Loyalty to Christ

The Scriptures call all people everywhere to repent and put faith in Christ. Repentance is not mere regret; it is a change of mind and direction, a turning to Jehovah's standards. Faith is not mere agreement; it is trust that results in obedience. Christ's sacrifice is sufficient, but it is not applied to those who reject Jehovah's authority. Salvation is offered broadly, but it is experienced personally by those who respond.

The Future Grounded in the Sacrifice: Resurrection and Righteous Life

The Hope of Resurrection for the Dead

Because death ends personhood, the resurrection hope is precious. Jehovah will restore life, and Christ's ransom ensures that resurrected humans can be reconciled to God. This is the ultimate hope for fallen humanity: not escape into disembodied existence, but restored life under Jehovah's righteous rule.

The Restoration of Jehovah's Purpose Through the Redeemer

Christ's sacrifice is tied to Jehovah's original purpose for earth. Redemption serves restoration. The atonement opens the way for a righteous human society on earth, free from the domination of sin and death. Christ, as King, will rule to remove wickedness and establish justice. Those who obey will enjoy the blessings Jehovah intended from the beginning.

CHAPTER 12 Salvation as a Path and Journey with the Heavenly Hope and the Earthly Hope

Salvation in Scripture: A Lived Path Under Jehovah's Authority

Scripture presents salvation as a lived path, not a static condition that cannot be lost. This does not mean salvation is earned by human effort. It means salvation is experienced as ongoing faithfulness—repentance, obedience, endurance, and growth—grounded in Christ's sacrifice and directed by the Spirit-inspired Word. The New

Testament repeatedly calls believers to continue, to endure, to remain, to hold fast, and to work out salvation with fear of displeasing Jehovah. These commands are meaningless if salvation is treated as an untouchable status gained once regardless of later rebellion.

Salvation is a journey because life is lived in a wicked world where Satan's influence, human imperfection, and demonic pressure aim to devour faith. The Christian path is guarded by Jehovah through His Word, supported by the congregation, and empowered by the hope set before us. That hope has two expressions in Scripture: a limited heavenly hope for those who will serve with Christ as kings, priests, and judges, and a broad earthly hope for the righteous who will inherit eternal life on a restored paradise earth, fulfilling Jehovah's original purpose.

The Foundation of the Journey: Faith in Christ and Repentance Toward Jehovah

The Entry Point Is Grace, Not Merit

No one begins the salvation path by personal goodness. All have sinned. Forgiveness comes through Christ's sacrifice. The believer is reconciled to Jehovah by grace through faith. Yet the New Testament's emphasis on grace never cancels the call to obedience. Grace establishes the relationship; obedience expresses loyalty within the relationship. A living faith produces action, not as payment, but as the fruit of genuine trust.

Repentance as a Change of Direction

Repentance is not a momentary emotion. It is a moral turning. The believer rejects former patterns and embraces Jehovah's standards. This includes sexual purity, honesty, peaceableness, refusal of idolatry, and love for neighbor. The salvation path has a visible direction. The believer does not drift; he follows Christ.

Salvation as Continuing: Warnings and Exhortations in the New Testament

The Real Possibility of Falling Away

Scripture warns believers against hardening the heart, returning to sinful lifestyles, loving the present world, and abandoning the faith. Such warnings are not theatrical. They function as real guardrails. Jehovah treats believers as responsible moral agents who must endure. The Christian life is therefore a race that must be finished, a fight that must be completed, and a faith that must be guarded.

Assurance Rooted in Jehovah's Faithfulness and Human Endurance

Biblical assurance is not arrogance. It is confidence grounded in Jehovah's character and in the believer's present pattern of faith and obedience. The Christian can have strong confidence because Jehovah is faithful, Christ's sacrifice is sufficient, and the Scriptures provide clear guidance. Yet Scripture also calls for self-examination and continuing loyalty. Salvation is a path in which Jehovah supplies everything needed, and the believer must respond with perseverance.

Edward D. Andrews

The Heavenly Hope: A Limited Number Serving With Christ

Kingship, Priesthood, and Judgment With Christ

The New Testament presents a group who will reign with Christ. Their role is governmental and priestly: administering righteous rule, applying the benefits of the atonement, and participating in judgment in harmony with Christ. This is not a vague honorific. It is a functional assignment within Jehovah's purpose. Christ is King, and He shares authority with those who will rule with Him.

This heavenly group is described as "called" to reign, to judge, and to serve as priests. Their work supports the restoration of righteous life among humanity. Their authority is not independent; it is under Christ, in full submission to Jehovah's will.

The Limited Number and the Nature of Their Calling

Scripture presents this heavenly group as limited in number. Revelation's presentation of 144,000 is not framed as an indefinite crowd but as a counted group, distinct from the great crowd also described. The point is not to promote curiosity or pride, but to honor the clarity of Scripture: Jehovah has designed an administrative arrangement under Christ for the coming kingdom.

Those with the heavenly hope are not superior Christians by personal worth. All salvation depends on Christ. Rather, their hope reflects an assigned role. Their lives on earth are marked by faithfulness, moral purity, and steadfast loyalty to Jehovah and Christ. They are prepared for service, not self-exaltation.

Roles and Responsibilities of Those in Heaven

Serving Under Christ for the Blessing of Humanity

The heavenly rulers serve for the benefit of others. Their kingship is not exploitation; it is righteous leadership. Their priesthood is not ritualism; it is mediating the application of Christ's sacrifice so that humanity can be restored fully. Their judging is not harshness; it is the establishment of justice, the exposure of evil, and the protection of righteousness.

Unity With Jehovah's Purpose for Earth

Heavenly service is not the replacement of earth's purpose but the means by which earth's purpose is accomplished. The kingdom government is directed toward restoring the world to righteousness. The heavenly hope therefore harmonizes with the earthly hope. One is administrative; the other is the lived outcome for redeemed humanity.

The Earthly Hope: Eternal Life on Paradise Earth

Returning to the Original Purpose

From Genesis onward, Jehovah's purpose includes humans living on earth, cultivating it, and enjoying peaceful life under His standards. The promise that the righteous will live forever on the earth is not an isolated statement. It is a consistent thread. The earthly hope is the fulfillment of the creation mandate in a cleansed world where wickedness is removed and righteousness is secure.

This hope is intensely practical. It means family life ordered by love and truth, meaningful work free from futility, worship without persecution, and life without the domination of sickness and death. It is not a fantasy built on sentiment. It is the direct outcome of Jehovah's declared intention to have an inhabited earth filled with righteous people.

Resurrection and Life Restored

Because death is cessation of personhood, the earthly hope includes resurrection. Jehovah will restore the dead to life. The ransom makes this possible by removing sin's legal barrier. Resurrected humans will have the opportunity to learn righteousness under Christ's rule. The earth becomes the home of a renewed humanity, not a graveyard of failed history.

One Salvation, Two Hopes, One Unified Purpose

Distinction Without Division

The heavenly hope and the earthly hope are distinct, but they are not competing. Both are grounded in the same Christ, the same ransom, the same Jehovah, and the same Scriptures. The difference lies in assignment and destiny. Some are appointed to serve in the heavenly government with Christ; the rest of the righteous receive everlasting life on earth under that government. This preserves the integrity of Jehovah's original purpose and the explicit promises concerning the earth.

Christian Identity Shaped by Hope and Faithfulness

A Christian's identity is not anchored in self-chosen destiny but in submission to Jehovah's will. The believer's calling is to faithfulness now: obedience to Scripture, participation in congregational life, evangelism, moral purity, and endurance. The Spirit guides through the Word. The believer's path is steady when it is Scriptural, not when it is driven by personal ambition.

The Journey's Daily Shape: Walking Worthily of the Calling

Scripture as the Map for the Path

Since the Holy Spirit guides through the Spirit-inspired Word, the salvation journey is sustained by regular Scripture intake: reading, study, meditation, and application. This produces discernment and stability. It also protects against doctrinal drift and moral compromise. The believer learns to think biblically, to choose wisely, and to endure pressure without abandoning loyalty to Jehovah.

Works as Evidence, Not Currency

Obedience is not a payment for salvation. It is evidence of living faith. Christians are created for good works, and those works demonstrate allegiance to Christ. Love, holiness, generosity, truthfulness, and courage under pressure are the visible fruit of the salvation path. Where such fruit is absent and unrepentant sin dominates, the claim of salvation is exposed as empty.

The Kingdom Hope and the Christian's Present Mission

Evangelism as Required of All Christians

Jehovah's purpose includes gathering people into the way of salvation. Christians are commanded to preach and teach. Evangelism is not reserved for a few. It is the calling of all believers according to their ability and circumstance. This mission is fueled by love for neighbor and loyalty to Christ, and it is guided by Scripture, not by private revelations.

Endurance Until Christ's Return and the Thousand Years

Scripture presents Christ's return before the thousand-year reign, during which His kingdom rule advances Jehovah's purpose. The believer's focus is therefore endurance and faithfulness. Salvation is a path walked to the end. Jehovah supplies hope, truth, and strength through His Word, and believers respond with steadfast loyalty.

CHAPTER 13 Living in Anticipation: Preparing for the New Heavens and Earth

The Sure Promise of a Renewed Creation

Scripture does not present the future hope as an escape from creation but as creation restored and brought to its intended goal under the reign of the Messiah. The prophets spoke of "new heavens and a new earth" in language that anchors hope in real life, real justice, real peace, and real worship centered on Jehovah. Isaiah records Jehovah's promise: "For look! I am creating new heavens and a new earth; and the former things will not be remembered, nor will they come to mind" (Isa. 65:17). The point is not amnesia as though God erases meaning, but the end of what corrupts life—violence, oppression, sickness, grief, and death—so thoroughly that the weight of the former world no longer governs the hearts of the redeemed.

When Peter later speaks of "new heavens and a new earth in which righteousness dwells" (2 Pet. 3:13), he draws on that prophetic promise and places it within the timeline of Christ's return and God's decisive intervention. "Righteousness dwells" means righteousness has a home there; it is not an occasional visitor. In the present world, righteousness is opposed, mocked, and pressured. In the new world, righteousness is the atmosphere. The moral order that sin destabilized is permanently reestablished, not by human progress but by divine action grounded in Christ's atoning sacrifice and Jehovah's faithfulness to His Word.

The book of Revelation depicts the same reality in vivid, covenantal language: "Look! The tent of God is with mankind, and he will dwell with them, and they will be his peoples" (Rev. 21:3). The phrase "with mankind" presses the promise into the realm of embodied human life. God's purpose is not simply to relocate people; it is to dwell with them in a cleansed creation, with all rival powers removed and all rebellion ended.

The Promise of a Renewed Creation

New Heavens and New Earth in Context

A careful, historical-grammatical reading recognizes that biblical writers use "heavens and earth" as a comprehensive way of describing the created order, including the structures of human society under spiritual influence. When Scripture announces a "new" heavens and earth, it is announcing a new order—creation liberated from corruption and human society reordered under the righteous King.

This matches Paul's teaching that creation was "subjected to futility" and "will be set free from its slavery to corruption" (Rom. 8:20-21). The problem is not matter itself, but corruption, decay, and sin's dominion within the present order.

The promise also maintains continuity: the earth remains the proper home for humanity as God designed it. The opening chapters of Genesis present the earth as a purposeful environment for human life, with humans made in God's image to exercise stewardship under His authority. That original intention is not discarded. It is recovered and perfected through Christ, the last Adam, who succeeds where Adam failed and secures the restoration of what was lost.

The End of Death and the Removal of Wickedness

Revelation declares, "Death will be no more, neither will mourning nor outcry nor pain be anymore" (Rev. 21:4). Death is not treated as a friend or a doorway; it is an enemy that entered through sin and is abolished through Christ's victory. The abolition of death requires more than comfort; it requires judgment. Scripture consistently ties the hope of a world without death to the removal of those who cling to wickedness and refuse God's rule. This is not cruelty but moral necessity. A world where righteousness truly dwells cannot be sustained if rebellion is allowed to continue indefinitely.

The final plan includes the complete exposure and removal of Satan's influence. Humanity's deepest wounds are not only internal; they are aggravated by a malicious spiritual adversary. The new world is the world after Satan's deceit is ended, after his accusations are silenced, and after the conditions that foster corruption are removed. God's love is not sentimental; it is holy, and holiness requires a final cleansing.

Our Role in the New Creation

Living Now as Citizens of the Coming Order

The promise of renewal is not given to fuel passive waiting. Peter makes the ethical force of the promise explicit: since these things are to occur, "what sort of persons ought you to be in holy conduct and godly devotion" (2 Pet. 3:11). The future order calls forth present holiness. This is not holiness as withdrawal from people, but holiness as separation from sin and dedication to Jehovah's will in the midst of a crooked world.

Jesus trained His disciples to pray, "Let your Kingdom come. Let your will take place, as in heaven, also on earth" (Matt. 6:10). That prayer is not abstract; it reorients daily life. If God's will is the defining reality of the coming world, then the disciple prepares by choosing that will now—inside the home, at work, in speech, in integrity, and in mercy. A Christian does not pretend perfection. A Christian practices repentance and obedience because the coming world is the world where God's will is done with joy and without resistance.

Evangelism as Participation in Jehovah's Saving Purpose

The new heavens and earth will be populated by those reconciled to God through Christ. The risen Christ commanded the making of disciples and the teaching of obedience to all He commanded (Matt. 28:19-20). Evangelism is therefore not optional and not a mere program. It is participation in Jehovah's saving purpose, calling imperfect humans to repentance, baptism, and the path of obedient faith that leads to life.

In a world saturated with despair, the good news is not a vague optimism; it is the announcement that Jehovah has acted decisively in

Christ, that sin can be forgiven, that conscience can be cleansed, and that life can be redirected toward the coming order. Christians proclaim this not as moral superiority but as rescued sinners pointing to the Rescuer.

Congregational Life as Training for the Coming World

The congregation is a present expression of the future order in miniature. It is not perfect, because it is made of imperfect people. Yet it is designed to cultivate truth, love, discipline, and mutual strengthening by the Spirit-inspired Scriptures. The new world will be characterized by pure worship and righteous relationships. Congregational life trains believers to forgive, to reconcile, to speak truthfully, to bear burdens, and to submit to Christ's authority.

This also includes maintaining biblical patterns of qualified male shepherding and teaching in the assembly, not as a cultural relic but as obedience to apostolic instruction. The coming world is not defined by human trends, but by God's revealed order. Living in anticipation means ordering the church according to Christ's instructions rather than reshaping it to fit the spirit of the age.

Anticipating the Full Realization of Redemption's Goal

Redemption Aims at Restored Human Life Under God

Redemption is not merely the cancellation of guilt; it is the restoration of humans to life with God as He intended. Scripture holds together forgiveness, transformation, and future inheritance. Believers are reconciled now, disciplined now, and trained now for life in the coming righteous world. This is why the New Testament speaks of salvation as something believers have received and something they will receive. The Christian is already forgiven in Christ, yet still must endure, obey, and remain faithful.

This forward-looking posture guards against two errors. One error is despair: imagining that the world's brokenness is the final word. The other error is complacency: imagining that forgiveness removes the need for vigilance. The apostolic writings do not allow either. The hope of renewal strengthens endurance and fuels holiness precisely because God's future is certain.

The Place of the Heavenly Rulers and the Earthly Inheritance

The New Testament teaches that Christ will rule and that He will have co-rulers. Revelation speaks of those who will "reign on the earth" (Rev. 5:10) and depicts a distinct group "bought from the earth" in a special sense (Rev. 14:1-3). Scripture also presents the broader hope of the meek inheriting the earth (Matt. 5:5) and of righteous humanity living under God's Kingdom government. This harmonizes the biblical picture: a select group rules with Christ in heaven as part of the Kingdom administration, while the redeemed of humankind enjoy everlasting life on a restored earth under that righteous reign.

Anticipation, then, is not a fuzzy dream of clouds, but a concrete expectation: God's government through Christ will bring the earth into alignment with His will, and human life will flourish as intended.

The Beauty and Majesty of God's Final Plan

Jehovah's final plan is majestic because it vindicates His holiness, fulfills His promises, and satisfies the deepest longings He placed within humanity for life, peace, and righteousness. The beauty of the plan is also moral beauty. God does not ignore evil; He defeats it. He does not excuse sin; He provides atonement. He does not abandon imperfect humans; He calls them to Himself through Christ, cleanses them, disciplines them, and leads them forward on a path that ends in life.

Living in anticipation means letting that coming world press upon the present. It means allowing the promise to shape priorities, speech, habits, and loves. The Christian's hope is not wishful thinking; it is anchored in Jehovah's oath and in the finished ransom accomplished by Jesus Christ.

CHAPTER 14 Embracing Our Imperfection, Holding onto Hope

The Journey of Faith and Imperfection

The Bible never flatters human nature. It tells the truth: humans are fallen, conscience is damaged, desires are disordered, and even sincere believers feel the pull of sin. Yet Scripture also refuses despair, because Jehovah has acted in Christ to forgive, to cleanse, and to train imperfect people for life. The Christian life is therefore not a performance for God but a journey with God, grounded in grace and expressed in obedience.

Paul describes the inner conflict of the believer with striking honesty. He can delight in God's law in his inner man and still feel another principle in his members warring against that delight (Rom. 7:22-23). This is not permission to sin; it is an explanation of why vigilance is necessary. Imperfection does not disappear the moment a person believes. The believer must learn to hate sin, confess it, resist it, and replace it with righteousness. This is why the New Testament repeatedly speaks in terms of putting off and putting on, of being renewed, of being transformed by truth.

At the same time, the believer does not carry this burden alone. Jehovah provides the Scriptures, the congregation, prayer, and the example and authority of Jesus Christ. The Christian is not expected to manufacture righteousness from within. He is expected to submit to God's Word, to repent when he falls, and to walk forward in faithful obedience.

Strengthening Our Relationship With God

Approaching Jehovah with Reverence and Confidence

A believer's relationship with Jehovah is both reverent and confident. Reverent, because God is holy and sin is deadly serious. Confident, because Jesus is a High Priest who can sympathize with our weakness and because His ransom is sufficient for real forgiveness. Hebrews urges believers to approach "the throne of grace" to receive mercy and find help at the right time (Heb. 4:16). The language is relational: throne, grace, mercy, help. Jehovah is not distant. He is accessible through Christ.

This confidence does not rest on self-esteem or self-approval. It rests on the character of God and on the atonement provided by His

Son. When believers pray, they do not bargain with God or demand. They confess, they ask, they thank, they seek wisdom, and they submit. Prayer becomes a practical way of refusing the lie that sin is stronger than God's mercy.

Letting the Spirit-Inspired Word Do Its Work

Jehovah's guidance comes through the Holy Spirit-inspired Word, not through a mystical indwelling. Scripture is living and active; it exposes motives, corrects thinking, and trains the conscience (Heb. 4:12; 2 Tim. 3:16-17). A believer strengthens his relationship with God by becoming saturated with the Bible—reading it, meditating on it, and obeying it. This is not mere information. It is communion through truth. God speaks in His Word, and the believer responds in faith and obedience.

A consistent pattern emerges in Scripture: those who drift from God drift first from His words. They neglect them, reinterpret them to suit desires, or treat them as optional. The opposite is also true: those who grow in hope and stability are those who treat Scripture as authoritative and sufficient for life and godliness.

Repentance as a Lifelong Posture

Repentance is not a single moment at the beginning of Christian life; it is a continuing posture. John writes to believers, "If we confess our sins, he is faithful and righteous to forgive us our sins and to cleanse us from all unrighteousness" (1 John 1:9). Confession is not self-hatred. It is agreement with God about sin and a decisive turning away from it. The believer refuses to rename sin as personality or preference. He calls it what God calls it and turns from it.

This ongoing repentance deepens the relationship with Jehovah because it cultivates honesty. A believer learns not to hide. He learns to bring his failures into the light, where mercy and correction operate. This is how hope stays alive: not by pretending strength, but by depending on God's strength.

Remaining Steadfast in Hope and Anticipation

Hope Rooted in God's Promises, Not in Circumstances

Christian hope is not optimism about human society. It is confidence that Jehovah keeps His promises and that Christ will complete His work. Circumstances fluctuate. The world is often cruel. Human imperfection produces pain, conflict, and disappointment. Satan and demons exploit weakness and spread lies. If hope depends on circumstances, it will collapse. If hope depends on Jehovah's word, it will endure.

Paul calls the hope "an anchor for the soul" (Heb. 6:19). Biblically, a human is a soul; the point is that hope stabilizes the whole person. It prevents drift. It keeps the believer from being carried away by fear, cynicism, or sinful escapes.

Fighting Sin Without Falling Into Despair

The New Testament commands believers to wage war against the flesh and to resist the Devil. That fight is real, and believers sometimes stumble. The difference between the hypocrite and the faithful believer is not that one never sins; it is that one refuses repentance while the other returns to God again and again.

Scripture also guards believers against despair by reminding them that the Christian life is a path. A path includes steps, slips, corrections, and renewed effort. A believer learns to examine himself without self-destruction. He learns to hate sin without hating the possibility of God's mercy. He learns to accept discipline as an expression of God's fatherly love, not as rejection.

The Fellowship of the Congregation

God does not design Christians to endure alone. The congregation is a means of strengthening—teaching, encouragement, accountability, and love in practical forms. Isolation often magnifies temptation and distorts perspective. Fellowship helps believers remember the truth, confess struggles, and receive help. It also provides opportunities to serve, which pulls believers out of inward obsession and into outward love.

Steadfast hope grows when believers worship, learn, and serve alongside others who share the same promise of the coming Kingdom. This is part of anticipating God's future: living now as a people shaped by that future.

The Ultimate Fulfillment of God's Promise

Jehovah's promise culminates in a world where righteousness is not fragile and where God's people are not constantly beset by inner corruption and external deception. That fulfillment is not earned by human effort; it is granted through Christ. Yet it is entered by those who repent, believe, obey, and endure.

The believer holds onto hope by returning repeatedly to what God has said. He remembers that Jesus died for sinners, not for the self-sufficient, and that mercy is real. He remembers that the coming world is certain and that every act of obedience now is aligned with the world that will be. He remembers that Jehovah is not merely forgiving but transforming, teaching His people to walk in holiness as they await the full realization of His purpose.

Edward D. Andrews

CHAPTER 15 Receiving the Benefit of Christ's Death: Repentance, Baptism, and the Life of Obedient Faith

Christ's Death and the Ransom That Opens the Way

The New Testament presents Jesus' death as a ransom, an atoning sacrifice that truly addresses guilt and restores fellowship with God. Sin is not a minor flaw; it is rebellion against the Creator, producing real moral debt and real corruption. Jehovah's justice does not pretend sin is harmless. Yet His love provides the remedy: "Christ died for our sins according to the Scriptures" (1 Cor. 15:3). The ransom is not a vague symbol. It is God's appointed means to forgive, cleanse, and reconcile sinners.

To receive the benefit of Christ's death, a person must respond as Scripture commands. The Bible does not teach that mere acknowledgment of facts saves, nor does it teach that a one-time emotional decision guarantees future life regardless of later choices. It teaches a living faith expressed in repentance, baptism, and ongoing obedience. Salvation is a path, not a label.

Repentance That Turns the Whole Life

Repentance as a Decisive Turning

Repentance in Scripture is not regret alone. It is a change of mind that produces a change of direction. The repentant sinner agrees with Jehovah about sin, rejects it, and turns to God's rule. When Peter preached at Pentecost, the question was direct: "What are we to do?" Peter answered: "Repent, and let each one of you be baptized in the name of Jesus Christ for forgiveness of your sins" (Acts 2:37-38). Repentance is the first response because it confronts the root issue: the sinner must stop defending sin and begin submitting to God.

Repentance includes abandoning known sin, seeking forgiveness, and accepting Christ as Lord in the practical sense—His teachings define what is right, not personal preference. Repentance also includes a willingness to make restitution where possible, to confess wrongdoing where necessary, and to repair relationships as far as righteousness allows.

Faith That Trusts and Obeys

Biblical faith is not passive. It trusts Jehovah's promise in Christ and therefore obeys Jehovah's commands. James states the principle plainly: faith without works is dead (Jas. 2:17). He is not saying works earn salvation as wages. He is saying living faith is recognizable by obedience. If a person claims to trust Christ while refusing Christ's commands, that claim is empty.

This is why Jesus ties discipleship to hearing and doing: the wise man builds on the rock by doing His words (Matt. 7:24). The obedient life is not perfectionism; it is allegiance. The believer falls at times, but he does not make peace with sin.

Baptism by Immersion into Christ

Baptism as the God-Appointed Entry Point

The New Testament consistently presents baptism as the normal, commanded response of repentant believers. It is not an infant ritual and not a mere symbol detached from salvation. It is the public, embodied act of identifying with Christ's death and resurrection and entering the disciple's life. Paul teaches that those baptized into Christ were baptized into His death, so that they might walk in newness of life (Rom. 6:3-4). The logic is covenantal and moral: baptism marks a break with the old life and the start of a new one.

Because baptism is tied to repentance and faith, it must be for those able to understand and respond to the gospel. Infant baptism contradicts the New Testament pattern, which assumes personal repentance, confession, and commitment.

The Name of the Father, Son, and Holy Spirit

Jesus commanded baptism "in the name of the Father and of the Son and of the Holy Spirit" (Matt. 28:19). This does not mean mystical words guarantee salvation. It means the baptized person is entering a relationship of submission to the Father's authority, to the Son's lordship, and to the Holy Spirit's work as expressed in the Spirit-inspired Word. Baptism is therefore not magic; it is covenantal obedience.

Salvation as a Journey of Obedient Faith

Continuing in Christ Rather Than Drifting

The New Testament frequently warns believers against drifting, hardening the heart, or returning to deliberate sin. These warnings only make sense if the Christian life involves endurance. Hebrews urges believers to "hold firmly" and not fall away through unbelief (Heb. 3:12-14). This is not fear-mongering; it is realism. Imperfection remains a battlefront, and Satan seeks to devour. A Christian must remain watchful, feeding on truth and resisting sin.

Endurance is not grim determination. It is sustained trust expressed in continued obedience: continuing in prayer, continuing in Scripture, continuing in fellowship, continuing in moral seriousness.

Daily Obedience in Ordinary Life

Receiving the benefit of Christ's death shows itself in the daily habits of a disciple. The believer learns to speak truthfully, to control anger, to reject sexual immorality, to practice honesty, to forgive, to work diligently, and to love others in tangible ways. None of this is performed to impress God. It is the fruit of repentance and the outworking of faith.

Obedience also involves resisting the subtle sins that flourish in secrecy: pride, envy, bitterness, greedy craving, and rationalized dishonesty. These sins are not harmless; they corrode the conscience. The gospel calls for a clean heart, not merely a respectable exterior.

Confession, Correction, and Returning to the Path

Because salvation is a journey, the disciple must learn what to do when he stumbles. Scripture does not say believers never sin; it says they must not practice sin as a settled way of life. When a believer sins, he must confess, turn, seek reconciliation, and resume obedience. This keeps the conscience tender and prevents the heart from hardening.

Jehovah's forgiveness is not a license to repeat sin. It is a mercy that restores the repentant and strengthens the resolve to walk in holiness. The ransom is sufficient, but it is received by those who remain in repentant, obedient faith.

Evangelism and Good Works as Fruit, Not Currency

A disciple's life also includes active love and witness. Christians are commanded to make disciples, to proclaim the good news, and to do good to others. These works do not purchase salvation. They express the reality of faith. A forgiven sinner who understands mercy becomes a messenger of mercy.

In all of this, the center remains Christ. The believer does not trust his performance; he trusts the Savior and therefore obeys the Savior. That is how the sinner truly lays hold of the ransom: repentance, baptism, and a life that keeps walking in the light.

Edward D. Andrews

CHAPTER 16 Death, Resurrection, and Judgment: What Scripture Actually Promises to Imperfect Humans

A Clear Biblical Anthropology: What a Human Is

The Bible's teaching about hope cannot be separated from what the Bible teaches about human nature. Scripture does not teach that humans possess an immortal soul that survives death by nature. It

HUMAN IMPERFECTION

teaches that a human is a soul. Genesis states: "Jehovah God formed the man from the dust of the ground and breathed into his nostrils the breath of life, and the man became a living soul" (Gen. 2:7). The man did not receive a soul as a separable entity; he became a living soul, a living person.

This matters because it clarifies what death is. If man is a soul, death is the end of the person's conscious life. Scripture repeatedly describes death as returning to dust and losing conscious thought. "His spirit goes out, he returns to the ground; in that day his thoughts perish" (Ps. 146:4). Ecclesiastes says, "The dead know nothing" and "there is no work nor planning nor knowledge nor wisdom in Sheol, where you are going" (Eccl. 9:5, 10). These are not poetic exaggerations; they are doctrinally consistent statements about the nature of death.

What Death Is: Cessation, Not a Second Life Elsewhere

Sheol and Hades as the Grave

In the Old Testament, Sheol is the realm of the dead, the grave, gravedom. In the New Testament, Hades corresponds to that same reality. Scripture portrays both as the condition and place of the dead, not a realm of conscious torment for the wicked or conscious bliss for the righteous. That is why Revelation can speak of "death and Hades" giving up the dead in them (Rev. 20:13). If Hades were a place of ongoing conscious experience, the language of "giving up the dead" would be incoherent. The dead are there because they are dead.

This also preserves the biblical weight of resurrection. If the righteous were already fully alive in heaven, resurrection would be an unnecessary appendage. Yet the New Testament treats resurrection as essential, as the decisive act of God that restores life. Paul says that if there is no resurrection, faith is futile (1 Cor. 15:14-18). The hope is not disembodied survival; it is resurrection.

Why This Teaching Strengthens Hope for Imperfect People

For imperfect humans, the truth about death is sobering but also clarifying. Death is not a hidden continuation of suffering. It is the end of conscious life until God restores life by resurrection. This means the believer's comfort is not based on imagining the dead are presently enjoying their reward, but on the certainty that Jehovah remembers, that Christ has authority over death, and that resurrection is real.

What Resurrection Is: God Restoring Life by Re-creation

Resurrection as Restoration of the Person

Resurrection in Scripture is God's act of bringing the person back to life. Because death ends conscious existence, resurrection must be God's restoration of the whole person, including identity and memory. Jehovah's perfect knowledge secures personal continuity. The resurrected one is not a different person with a copied personality; he is the person restored by God's power and faithfulness.

Jesus taught a future resurrection as a real event: "The hour is coming when all who are in the tombs will hear his voice and come out" (John 5:28-29). Tombs, voice, come out—this is concrete. It is not a metaphor for spiritual awakening. It is the reversal of death.

The Order of Resurrection and the Millennial Reign

Scripture presents Christ returning before the 1,000-year reign. Revelation describes those who share in the "first resurrection" and reign with Christ for a thousand years (Rev. 20:4-6). This aligns with the biblical teaching that a select group rules with Christ in the heavenly administration of the Kingdom, while the broader redeemed humanity benefits from that righteous reign on earth.

The 1,000-year reign is not an optional detail; it is part of how Jehovah's purpose is carried out in history. It is the period in which Christ's Kingdom government applies the benefits of His ransom, brings the earth into full alignment with God's will, and leads humanity into the conditions promised in the prophets: peace, justice, and true worship.

Edward D. Andrews

Judgment and Accountability: How God Deals With Imperfect Humans

Judgment According to Deeds and Light Received

Revelation portrays the dead being judged "according to their deeds" (Rev. 20:12-13). This does not contradict salvation by grace; it explains the basis of accountability. Deeds reveal what a person truly loved, trusted, and obeyed. The New Testament also teaches degrees of accountability based on knowledge and opportunity. Jesus spoke of greater responsibility where greater light has been given (Luke 12:47-48). Jehovah is perfectly just. He does not judge with ignorance. He judges with complete knowledge of motives, opportunities, and choices.

For imperfect humans, this means judgment is not arbitrary. It also means that claiming ignorance is not a safe refuge if the person has resisted truth, loved darkness, or harmed others without repentance. Mercy is real, and so is justice.

The Role of Christ as Judge and Savior

The Father has entrusted judgment to the Son (John 5:22). This is profound comfort because the Judge is also the One who gave His life as a ransom for sinners. Christ understands human weakness without excusing sin. He knows what it means to be tempted, yet He never sinned. He is therefore qualified to judge righteously and to apply mercy where repentance is genuine.

This does not mean judgment is lenient toward stubborn wickedness. Scripture teaches final accountability and the removal of those who refuse Jehovah's rule. But it does mean that repentant sinners are not crushed by fear. They are called to repentance, obedience, and endurance, trusting the sufficiency of Christ's sacrifice.

Gehenna as Eternal Destruction, Not Eternal Torment

Jesus used Gehenna as a symbol of final, irreversible destruction. It is not a place where an immortal soul suffers forever. Scripture consistently teaches that the wages of sin is death (Rom. 6:23), not everlasting life in misery. Eternal punishment is eternal in its effect, not in ongoing conscious torment. The wicked are destroyed, not preserved forever.

This preserves the moral coherence of God's character. Jehovah does not perpetually sustain evil in conscious agony. He brings evil to an end. The final state is one where righteousness dwells, not one where evil is eternally quarantined but still alive.

The Promise That Anchors Hope

The Bible's promise to imperfect humans is not that imperfection is excused, but that forgiveness is available through Christ, that transformation is commanded and empowered by truth, that death will be undone by resurrection, and that judgment will be righteous and fair. The hope is not vague. It is structured: death is real, resurrection is real, judgment is real, and the coming world is real.

Jehovah's plan confronts the worst realities of human existence—sin and death—and answers them with a solution that is both just and merciful: the ransom of Christ, the resurrection of the dead, and the establishment of God's Kingdom over a renewed earth.

Edward D. Andrews

Other Books by Edward D. Andrews

Andrews, E. (2018). *THE EARLY CHRISTIAN COPYISTS OF THE NEW TESTAMENT: The Making and Copying of the New Testament Books.* Cambridge: Christian Publishing House.

Andrews, E. (2019). *Misrepresenting Jesus: Debunking Bart D. Ehrman's Misquoting Jesus [Fourth Edition].* Cambridge: Christian Publishing House.

Andrews, E. (2020). *FROM SPOKEN WORDS TO SACRED TEXTS: Introduction-Intermediate New Testament Textual Studies.* Cambridge: Christian Publishing House.

Andrews, E. D. (2011). *AN INTRODUCTION TO BIBLE DIFFICULTIES So-Called Errors and Contradictions.* Cambridge: Christian Publishing House.

Andrews, E. D. (2011). *BIBLE DIFFICULTIES: Debunking the Documentary Hypothesis.* Cambridge: Christian Publishing House.

Andrews, E. D. (2012). *An Introduction to Bible Difficulties: So-called Errors and Contradictions.* Cambridge, OH: Christian Publlishing House.

Andrews, E. D. (2012). *DIFFICULTIES IN THE BIBLE UPDATED: Updated and Expanded.* Cambridge, OH: Christian Publishing House.

Andrews, E. D. (2013). *BOOKS OF 2 JOHN 3 JOHN and JUDE CPH New Testament Commentary.* Cambridge: Christian Publishing House.

Andrews, E. D. (2015). *CRISIS OF FAITH: Saving Those Who Doubt* . Cambridge, OH: Christian Publishing House.

Andrews, E. D. (2015). *EVIDENCE THAT YOU ARE TRULY CHRISTIAN: Keep Testing Yourselves to See If You Are In the Faith - Keep Examining Yourselves.* Cambridge, OH: Christian Publishing House.

Andrews, E. D. (2016). *EXPLAINING THE DOCTRINE OF SALVATION: Basic Bible Doctrines of the Christian Faith.* Cambridge, OH: Christian Publishing House.

Andrews, E. D. (2016). *HOMOSEXUALITY - THE BIBLE AND THE CHRISTIAN: Basic Bible Doctrines of the Christian Faith.* Cambridge, OH: Christian Publishing House.

Andrews, E. D. (2016). *INTERPRETING THE BIBLE: Introduction to Biblical Hermeneutics.* Cambridge, OH: Christian Publishing House.

Andrews, E. D. (2016). *THE BATTLE FOR THE CHRISTIAN MIND: Be Transformed by the Renewal of Your Mind.* Cambridge, OH: Christian Publishing House.

Andrews, E. D. (2016). *THE CHRISTIAN APOLOGIST: Always Being Prepared to Make a Defense [Second Edition].* Cambridge, OH: Christian Publishing House.

Andrews, E. D. (2016). *THE COMPLETE GUIDE to BIBLE TRANSLATION: Bible Translation Choices and Translation Principles [Second Edition]* . Cambridge: Christian Publishing House.

Andrews, E. D. (2016). *THE EVANGELISM HANDBOOK: How All Christians Can Effectively Share God's Word in Their Community, [SECOND EDITION].* Cambridge, OH: Christian Publishing House.

Andrews, E. D. (2016). *THE SECOND COMING OF CHRIST: Basic Bible Doctrines of the Christian Faith.* Cambridge, OH: Christian Publishing House.

Andrews, E. D. (2016). *WHAT IS HELL?: Basic Bible Doctrines of the Christian Faith.* Cambridge, OH: Christian Publishing House.

Andrews, E. D. (2016). *YOUR GUIDE FOR DEFENDING THE BIBLE: Self-Education of the Bible Made Easy.* Cambridge, OH: Christian Publishing House.

Andrews, E. D. (2016). *YOUR WORD IS TRUTH: Being Sanctified In the Truth.* Cambridge, OH: Christian Publishing House.

Andrews, E. D. (2017). *CONVERSATIONAL EVANGELISM: Defending the Faith, Reasoning from the Scriptures, Explaining and Proving, Instructing in Sound Doctrine, and Overturning False Reasoning [Second Edition].* Cambridge, OH: Christian Publishing House.

Andrews, E. D. (2017). *DEFENDING OLD TESTAMENT AUTHORSHIP: The Word of God Is Authentic and True.* Cambridge, OH: Christian Publishing House.

Andrews, E. D. (2017). *EARLY CHRISTIANITY IN THE FIRST CENTURY: Jesus' Witnesses to the Ends of the Earth.* Cambridge, OH: Christian Publishing House.

Andrews, E. D. (2017). *FEARLESS: Be Courageous and Strong Through Your Faith In These Last Days.* Cambridge, OH: Christian Publishing House.

Andrews, E. D. (2017). *GOD WILL GET YOU THROUGH THIS: Hope and Help for Your Difficult Times.* Cambridge, OH: Christian Publishing House.

Andrews, E. D. (2017). *HOW TO STUDY YOUR BIBLE: Rightly Handling the Word of God.* Cambridge, OH: Christian Publishing House.

Andrews, E. D. (2017). *HUMAN IMPERFECTION: While We Were Sinners Christ Died For Us.* Cambridge, OH: Christian Ppublishing House.

Andrews, E. D. (2017). *HUSBANDS LOVE YOUR WIVES: How Should Husbands Treat Their Wives?* Cambridge, OH: Christian Publishing House.

Andrews, E. D. (2017). *IDENTIFYING THE ANTICHRIST: The Man of Lawlessness and the Mark of the Beast Revealed.* Cambridge, OH: Christian Publishing House.

Andrews, E. D. (2017). *IS THE BIBLE REALLY THE WORD OF GOD?: Is Christianity the One True Faith?* Cambridge, Ohio: Christian Publishing House.

Andrews, E. D. (2017). *IS THE QURAN THE WORD OF GOD?: Is Islam the One True Faith.* Cambridge, OH: Christian Publishing House.

Andrews, E. D. (2017). *IS THERE A REBEL IN THE HOUSE?: Youth Overcoming a Rebellious Heart.* Cambridge, OH: Christian Publishing House.

Andrews, E. D. (2017). *THE OUTSIDER: Coming-of-Age In This Moment.* Cambridge, OH: Christian Publishing House.

Andrews, E. D. (2017). *TURN OLD HABITS INTO NEW HABITS: Why and How the Bible Makes a Difference.* Cambridge, OH: Christian Publishing House.

Andrews, E. D. (2017). *WIVES BE SUBJECT TO YOUR HUSBANDS: How Should Wives Treat Their Husbands?* Cambridge, OH: Christian Publishing House.

Andrews, E. D. (2017). *YOU CAN MAKE A DIFFERENCE: Why and How Your Christian Life Makes a Difference.* Cambridge, OH: Christian Publishing House.

Andrews, E. D. (2018). *40 DAYS DEVOTIONAL FOR YOUTHS: Coming-of-Age In Christ.* Cambridge, OH: Christian Publishing House.

Andrews, E. D. (2018). *BLESSED BY GOD IN SATAN'S WORLD: How All Things Are Working for Your Good.* Cambridge, OH: Christian Publishing House.

Andrews, E. D. (2018). *CHRISTIAN APOLOGETIC EVANGELISM: Reaching Hearts with the Art of Persuasion.* Cambridge, OH: Christian Publishing House.

Andrews, E. D. (2018). *LET GOD USE YOU TO SOLVE YOUR PROBLEMS: GOD Will Instruct You and Teach You In the Way You Should Go.* Cambridge, OH: Christian Publishing House.

Andrews, E. D. (2018). *PROMISES OF GOD'S GUIDANCE: God Show Me Your Ways, Teach Me Your Paths, Guide Me In Your Truth and Teach Me.* Cambridge, OH: Christian Publishing House.

Andrews, E. D. (2018). *REASONABLE FAITH: Saving Those Who Doubt.* Cambridge, OH: Christian Publishing House.

Andrews, E. D. (2018). *REASONING FROM THE SCRIPTURES: Sharing CHRIST as You Help Others to Learn about the Mighty works of God.* Cambridge, Ohio: Christian Publishing House.

Andrews, E. D. (2018). *REASONING WITH THE WORLD'S VARIOUS RELIGIONS: Examining and Evangelizing Other Faiths.* Cambridge, OH: Christian Publishing House.

Andrews, E. D. (2018). *REVIEWING 2013 New World Translation of Jehovah's Witnesses: Examining the History of the Watchtower Translation and the Latest Revision.* Cambridge, OH: Christian Publishing House.

Andrews, E. D. (2018). *The CHURCH CURE: Overcoming Church Problems.* Cambridge, OH: Christian Publishing House.

Andrews, E. D. (2018). *THE KING JAMES BIBLE: Do You Know the King James Version?* Cambridge, OH: Christian Publishing House.

Andrews, E. D. (2018). *THE POWER OF GOD: The Word That Will Change Your Life Today.* Cambridge, OH: Christian Publishing House.

Andrews, E. D. (2018). *WHAT WILL HAPPEN IF YOU DIE?* Cambridge, OH: Christian Publishing House.

Andrews, E. D. (2018). *WHY ME?: When Bad Things Happen to Good People.* Cambridge, OH: Christian Publishing House.

Andrews, E. D. (2019). *400,000+ SCRIBAL ERRORS IN THE GREEK NEW TESTAMENT MANUSCRIPTS: What*

Assurance Do We Have that We Can Trust the Bible? Cambridge, OH: Christian Publishing House.

Andrews, E. D. (2019). *INTRODUCTION TO THE TEXT OF THE NEW TESTAMENT: From The Authors and Scribe to the Modern Critical Text.* Cambridge, Ohio: Christian Publishing House.

Andrews, E. D. (2019). *MIRACLES: What Does the Bible Really Teach?* Cambridge, OH: Christian Publishing House.

Andrews, E. D. (2019). *SATAN: Know Your Enemy.* Cambridge, OH: Christian Publishing House.

Andrews, E. D. (2019). *THE CHALLENGE OF TRANSLATING TRUTH: Bible Translation - No Easy Matter.* Cambridge, OH: Christian Publishing House.

Andrews, E. D. (2019). *THE READING CULTURE OF EARLY CHRISTIANITY: The Production, Publication, Circulation, and Use of Books in the Early Christian Church.* Cambridge, OH: Christian Publishing House.

Andrews, E. D. (2020). *INERRANCY OF SCRIPTURE: How Can We Believe Inerrancy of Scripture In the Originals When We Don't Have the Originals?* Cambridge, OH: Christian Publishing House.

Andrews, E. D. (2020). *THE BIBLICAL MARRIAGE: Biblical Counsel that Will Strengthen a Strong Marriage and Save a Failing Marriage.* Cambridge, OH: Christian Publishing House.

Andrews, E. D. (2020). *THE NEW TESTAMENT DOCUMENTS: Can They Be Trusted?* Cambridge, OH: Christian Publishing House.

Andrews, E. D. (2020). *THE P52 PROJECT: Is P52 Really the Earliest Greek New Testament Manuscript?* Cambridge, OH: Christian Publishing House.

Andrews, E. D. (2020). *WALK HUMBLY WITH YOUR GOD: Putting God's Purpose First in Your Life.* Cambridge, OH: Christian Publishing House.

Andrews, E. D. (2021). *THE 1946 PROJECT: The Supposed Mistranslation of "Homosexual" In 1 Corinthians 6:9.* Cambridge, OH: Christian Publishing House.

Andrews, E. D. (2022). *THE LETTER OF JAMES: An Apologetic and Background Exposition of the Holy Scriptures (CPH New Testament Commentary).* Cambridge, Ohio: Christian Publishing House.

Andrews, E. D. (2022). *THE ORIGINAL TEXT OF THE NEW TESTAMENT: Ascertaining the Original Words of the Original Greek New Testament Manuscripts.* Cambridge, OH: Christian Publishing House.

Andrews, E. D. (2022). *THE QUEST FOR THE HISTORICAL JESUS: Are Doubts About Jesus Justified?* Cambridge, OH: Christian Publishing House.

Andrews, E. D. (2023). *A JOURNEY THROUGH ANCIENT LETTER WRITING: A New Look at New Testament Letters in the Greco-Roman World.* Cambridge, OH: Christian Publishing House.

Andrews, E. D. (2023). *ARCHAEOLOGY & THE NEW TESTAMENT.* Cambridge, Ohio: Christian publishing House.

Andrews, E. D. (2023). *ARCHAEOLOGY & THE OLD TESTAMENT.* Cambridge, Ohio: Christian Publishing House.

Andrews, E. D. (2023). *BIBLICAL APOCALYPTICS HANDBOOK: A Study of the Most Important Revelations that God and Christ Disclosed in the Bible.* Cambridge, OH: Christian Publishing House.

Andrews, E. D. (2023). *BIBLICAL EXEGESIS: Biblical Criticism on Trial.* Cambridge, OH: Christian Publishing House.

Andrews, E. D. (2023). *CHRISTIAN APOLOGETICS: Answering the Tough Questions: Evidence and Reason in Defense of the Faith.* Cambridge, Ohio: Christian Publishing House.

Andrews, E. D. (2023). *DISCOVERING THE ORIGINAL BIBLE: Accuracy, Authenticity, and Reliability.* Cambridge, OH: Christian Publishing House.

Andrews, E. D. (2023). *FAITHFUL MINDS: A Biblical and Cognitive Behavioral Therapy Approach to Mental Health and Wellness.* Cambridge, OH: Christian Publishing House.

Andrews, E. D. (2023). *GOD'S OUTLAW: William Tyndale and the English Bible.* Cambridge, Ohio: Christian Publishing House.

Andrews, E. D. (2023). *HOW WE GOT THE BIBLE.* Cambridge, OH: Christian Publishing House.

Andrews, E. D. (2023). *INTRODUCTION TO OLD TESTAMENT TEXTUAL CRITICISM.* Cambridge, OH: Christian Publishing House.

Andrews, E. D. (2023). *INTRODUCTION TO THE TEXT OF THE OLD TESTAMENT: From the Authors and Scribes to the*

Modern Critical Text. Cambridge, OH: Christian Publishing House.

Andrews, E. D. (2023). *ISLAM & THE QURAN: Examining the Quran & Islamic Teachings.* Cambridge, OH: Christian Publishing House.

Andrews, E. D. (2023). *ISLAMIC ESCHATOLOGY: Awaiting Al-Mahdi—The Twelfth Imam and the Future of Islam.* Cambridge, OH: Christian Publishing House.

Andrews, E. D. (2023). *JOHN CALVIN: A Solitary Quest for the Truth.* Cambridge, Ohio: Christian Publishing House.

Andrews, E. D. (2023). *LIFE DOES HAVE A PURPOSE: Discovering and Living Your Ultimate Purpose.* Cambridge, OH: Christian Publishing House.

Andrews, E. D. (2023). *MARTIN LUTHER: The Man and His Legacy.* Cambridge, Ohio: Christian Publishing House.

Andrews, E. D. (2023). *MERE CHRISTIANITY REIMAGINED: Rediscovering the Faith for the 21st Century.* Cambridge, OH: Christian Publishing House.

Andrews, E. D. (2023). *THE BIBLE AS HISTORY: A Historical Journey Through the Bible.* Cambridge, Ohio: Christian Publishing House.

Andrews, E. D. (2023). *THE BIBLE ON TRIAL: Examining the Evidence for Being Inspired, Inerrant, Authentic, and True.* Cambridge, Ohio: Christian Publishing House.

Andrews, E. D. (2023). *THE BOOK OF PROVERBS Chapters 1-15: CPH Old Testament Commentary: Volume 17.* Cambridge, OH: Christian Publishing House.

Andrews, E. D. (2023). *THE BOOK OF PROVERBS Chapters 16-23: CPH Old Testament Commentary: Volume 18.* Cambridge, OH: Christian Publishing House.

Andrews, E. D. (2023). *THE EXPOSITORY DICTIONARY: A Companion Study Tool to the Updated American Standard Version.* Cambridge, OH: Christian Publishing House.

Andrews, E. D. (2023). *THE MACCABEES: The Hasmonaean Dynasty between Malachi and Matthew.* Cambridge, OH: Christian Publishing House.

Andrews, E. D. (2023). *THE NASB: Preserving Truth or Compromising Accuracy?: A Critical Look at the Shift from the 1995 to 2020 Editions of the New American Standard Bible (NASB).* Cambridge, OH: Christian Publishing House.

Andrews, E. D. (2023). *THE OLD TESTAMENT: Commentary, Background, & Bible Difficulties (Introduction to the Old Testament).* Cambridge, OH: Christian Publishing House.

Andrews, E. D. (2023). *THE SCRIBE AND THE TEXT OF THE NEW TESTAMENT: Scribal Activities in the Transmission of the Text of the New Testament.* Cambridge, Ohio: Christian Publishing House.

Andrews, E. D. (2023). *THE TEXT OF THE NEW TESTAMENT: A Beginners Handbook to New Testament Textual Studies.* Cambridge, OH: Christian Publishing House.

Andrews, E. D. (2023). *THE TEXTUS RECEPTUS: The "Received Text" of the New Testament.* Cambridge, OH: Christian Publishing House.

Andrews, E. D. (2023). *THE YOUNG CHRISTIAN'S SURVIVAL GUIDE: Common Questions Young Christians Are Asked* about God, the Bible, and the Christian Faith Answered (Defending Your Faith for Christian Youths). Cambridge, OH: Christian Publishing House.

Andrews, E. D. (2023). *Unlocking the Bible: A Beginner's Guide to the Coherence-Based Genealogical Method (CBGM): Understanding How Scholars Piece Together the New Testament.* Cambridge, OH: Christian Publishing House.

Andrews, E. D. (2023). *UNSHAKABLE BELIEFS: Strategies for Strengthening and Defending Your Faith.* Cambridge, OH: Christian Publishing House.

Andrews, E. D. (2023). *WOKEISM: The Predatory Grooming of Your Children.* Cambridge, OH: Christian Publishing House.

Andrews, E. D. (2024). *BATTLE PLANS: A Game Plan for Answering Objections to the Christian Faith.* Cambridge, OH: Christian Publishing House.

Andrews, E. D. (2024). *CHRISTIAN APOLOGISTS OF THE SECOND CENTURY: Christian Defenders of the Faith.* Cambridge, OH: Christian Publishing House.

Andrews, E. D. (2024). *CHRISTIAN THEOLOGY: The Christian's Ultimate Guide to Learning from the Bible.* Cambridge, OH: Christian Publishing House.

Andrews, E. D. (2024). *CREATION AND COSMOS: A Journey Through Creation, Science, and the Origins of Life.* Cambridge, OH: Christian Publishing House.

Andrews, E. D. (2024). *DO WE STILL NEED A LITERAL BIBLE?: Discover the Truth about Literal Bibles.* Cambridge, OH: Christian Publishing House.

Andrews, E. D. (2024). *FAITH UNDER FIRE: Refuting the Top 30 Arguments Atheists Make Against Christianity.* Cambridge, OH: Christian Publishing House.

Andrews, E. D. (2024). *HELL: All You Need to Know About Hell.* Cambridge, OH: Christian Publishing House.

Andrews, E. D. (2024). *INTRODUCTION TO HANDWRITING STYLES: Authenticating and Dating New Testament Manuscripts.* Cambridge, OH: Christian Publishing House.

Andrews, E. D. (2024). *MISGUIDED THINKING: Correct and Guide Your Thoughts in a Healthier Direction.* Cambridge, OH: Christian Publishing House.

Andrews, E. D. (2024). *REASON MEETS FAITH: Addressing and Refuting Atheism's Challenges to Christianity.* Cambridge, OH: Christian Publishing House.

Andrews, E. D. (2024). *THE BABYLONIAN EMPIRE.* Cambridge, OH: Christian Publishing House.

Andrews, E. D. (2024). *THE BATTLE OF JERICHO—Myth or Fact?* Cambridge, OH: Christian Publishing House.

Andrews, E. D. (2024). *THE DEAD SEA SCROLLS: What Is the Truth About the Dead Sea Scrolls?* Cambridge, OH: Christian Publishing House.

Andrews, E. D. (2024). *THE DIDACHE: The Teaching of the Twelve Apostles.* Cambridge, OH: Christian Publishing House.

Andrews, E. D. (2024). *THE ENCYCLOPEDIA OF CHRISTIAN APOLOGETICS: The Resource for Pastors, Teachers, and Believers.* Cambridge: Christian Publishing House.

Andrews, E. D. (2024). *THE HISTORICAL ADAM & EVE: Reconciling Faith and Fact in Genesis.* Cambridge, OH: Christian Publishing House.

Andrews, E. D. (2024). *THE HISTORICAL JESUS: The Death, Burial, and Resurrection of Jesus Christ.* Cambridge, OH: Christian Publishing House.

Andrews, E. D. (2024). *THE TEACHER OF RIGHTEOUSNESS AND THE WICKED PRIEST: Their Roles, Rivalry, Conflict, and Divine Judgment in the Dead Sea Scrolls.* Cambridge, OH: Christian Publishing House.

Andrews, E. D. (2024). *THE TRAINING OF THE TWELVE APOSTLES: Essential Lessons for Every Christian's Journey.* Cambridge, OH: Christian Publishing House.

Andrews, E. D. (2024). *UNDERSTANDING THE HITTITES: Biblical History, Archaeological Discoveries, and Etymological Clarifications.* Cambridge, OH: Christian Publishing House.

Andrews, E. D. (2025). *A FRESH LOOK AT PAUL'S THEOLOGY: Biblical Theology as Revealed through Paul.* Cambridge, OH: Christian Publishing House.

Andrews, E. D. (2025). *ATHEISM: What Will You Say to an Atheist.* Cambridge, OH: Christian Publishing House.

Andrews, E. D. (2025). *BIBLE DIFFICULTIES: How to Approach Difficulties In the Bible.* Cambridge, OH: Christian Publishing House.

Andrews, E. D. (2025). *BIBLICAL ARCHAEOLOGY: The Bible Beneath Our Feet.* Cambridge, OH: Christian Publishing House.

Andrews, E. D. (2025). *BIBLICAL WORDS AND THEIR MEANING: An Introduction to Lexical Semantics.* Cambridge, OH: Christian Publishing House.

Andrews, E. D. (2025). *BURIED SCRIPTURE: How the Roman Catholic Church Replaced God's Word with Tradition.* Cambridge, OH: Christian Publishing House.

Andrews, E. D. (2025). *CAN WE TRUST THE BIBLE?* Cambridge, OH: Christian Publishing House.

Andrews, E. D. (2025). *DISCOVERING GENESIS ANSWERS: Exploring the Historical and Cultural Contexts of Genesis, One Insight at a Time (Answers from Genesis).* Cambridge, OH: Christian Publishing House.

Andrews, E. D. (2025). *DISCOVERING GENESIS ANSWERS: Tackling Tough Questions in Genesis: One Solution at a Time (Answers from Genesis).* Cambridge, OH: Christian Publishing House.

Andrews, E. D. (2025). *DISCOVERING GENESIS ANSWERS: Unveiling the Truths of Creation, One Answer at a Time (Answers from Genesis).* Cambridge, OH: Christian Publishing House.

Andrews, E. D. (2025). *EARLY CHRISTIANITY: Exploring Backgrounds, Historical Settings, and Cultures.* Cambridge, OH: Christian Publishing House.

Andrews, E. D. (2025). *EARLY CHRISTIANITY: From Christ to Constantine.* Cambridge, OH: Christian Publishing House.

Andrews, E. D. (2025). *IMMORTALITY OF THE SOUL: The Birth of the Doctrine.* Cambridge, OH: Christian Publishing House.

Andrews, E. D. (2025). *ISLAMIC IDEOLOGICAL JIHAD: Islamic-Funded, Islamic-Indoctrinated, Western Youth.* Cambridge, OH: Christian Publishing House.

Andrews, E. D. (2025). *JEHOVAH OR YAHWEH: What Is the Correct Pronunciation of the Divine Name?* Cambridge, OH: Christian Publishing House.

Andrews, E. D. (2025). *JOSEPHUS & THE NEW TESTAMENT: Evidence from the First-Century Jewish Historian on Key Biblical Figures, Groups, and Events.* Cambridge, OH: Christian Publishing House.

Andrews, E. D. (2025). *LINGUISTICS AND THE BIBLICAL TEXT: Unlocking Scripture Through the Science of Language.* Cambridge, OH: Christian Publishing House.

Andrews, E. D. (2025). *MUHAMMAD: The Truth They Don't Want You to Know.* Cambridge, OH: Christian Publishing House.

Andrews, E. D. (2025). *OVERCOMING BIBLE DIFFICULTIES: Answers to the So-Called Errors and Contradictions [Second Edition].* Cambridge: Christian Publishing House.

Andrews, E. D. (2025). *PROVING GOD'S EXISTENCE.* Cambridge, OH: Christian Publishing House.

Andrews, E. D. (2025). *ROMAN CATHOLICISM: A Historical and Theological Refutation of a False Religion.* Cambridge, OH: Christian Publishing House.

Andrews, E. D. (2025). *THE ANDREWS BIBLE BLUEPRINT: Unlocking Scripture's Truth, History, and Wisdom.* Cambridge, OH: Christian Publishing House.

Andrews, E. D. (2025). *THE APOSTLE PAUL: Teacher, Preacher, Apologist, and Evangelist.* Cambridge, OH: Christian Publishing House.

Andrews, E. D. (2025). *THE EARLY VERSIONS OF THE NEW TESTAMENT: Their Origins, Transmission, and Reliability.* Cambridge, OH: Christian Publishing House.

Andrews, E. D. (2025). *THE EGYPTIAN EMPIRE: Its Role in Biblical History.* Cambridge, OH: Christian Publishing House.

Andrews, E. D. (2025). *THE ENCYCLOPEDIA OF THE TEXT OF THE NEW TESTAMENT: The Resource for Pastors, Teachers, and Believers.* Cambridge, OH: Christian Publishing House.

Andrews, E. D. (2025). *THE FACES OF ISLAM: Faith or Facade: Decoding Islam's Strategies.* Cambridge, OH: Christian Publishing House.

Andrews, E. D. (2025). *THE FALL OF AMERICA: A Biblical Warning for the Last Generation Before Armageddon.* Cambridge, OH: Christian Publishing House.

Andrews, E. D. (2025). *THE GUIDE TO SPIRITUAL WARFARE: Standing Firm in the Armor of God Against the Schemes of the Devil.* Cambridge, OH: Christian Publishing House.

Andrews, E. D. (2025). *THE LAST WATCHMAN: Standing for Truth in a Fallen World.* Cambridge, OH: Christian Publishing House.

Andrews, E. D. (2025). *THE OLD LATIN FRAGMENTS (VETUS LATINA): An Evangelical Scholarly Analysis.* Cambridge, OH: Christian Publishing House.

Andrews, E. D. (2025). *THE OLD TESTAMENT DOCUMENTS: Can They Be Trusted?* Cambridge, OH: Christian Publishing House.

Andrews, E. D. (2025). *THE RESTORATION OF THE ORIGINAL NEW TESTAMENT TEXTS: Ascertaining the Original Words of the Original Texts.* Cambridge, OH: Christian Publishing House.

Andrews, E. D. (2025). *THE STONES SPEAK: Biblical Archaeology and the Reliability of the Bible.* Cambridge, OH: Christian Publishing House.

Andrews, E. D. (2025). *THE WAR AGAINST THE TRUTH: Exposing the Lies That Allegedly Undermine the Christian Faith.* Cambridge, OH: Christian Publishing House.

Andrews, E. D. (2025). *TRUTH FROM THE DUST: Fresh Old Testament Archaeology Demonstrating the Reliability of God's Word.* Cambridge, OH: Christian Publishing House.

Andrews, E. D. (2025). *UNDERSTANDING BIBLICAL WORDS: A Guide to Sound Interpretation.* Cambridge, OH: Christian Publishing House.

Andrews, E. D. (2025). *WALKING IN THE LIGHT: Living a Set-Apart Life in a World of Darkness.* Cambridge, OH: Christian Publishing House.

Andrews, E. D. (2025). *WONDERFULLY MADE: Wonderful Are God's Works.* Cambridge, OH: Christian Publishing House.

Andrews, E. D. (2025). *YOUR YOUTH: The Young Christian's Guide to Making Right Choices.* Cambridge, OH: Christian Publishing House.

Andrews, E. D., & Farnell, F. D. (2017). *BIBLICAL CRITICISM: What are Some Outstanding Weaknesses of Modern Historical Criticism?* Cambridge, OH: Christian Publishing House.

Andrews, E. D., & Freeman, H. (2017). *THIRTEEN REASONS WHY YOU SHOULD KEEP LIVING: When Hope and Love Vanish.* Cambridge, OH: Christian Publishing House.

Andrews, E. D., & Marshall, T. F. (2023). *PAUL'S LETTER TO THE EPHESIANS: CPH New Testament Commentary.* Cambridge, OH: Christian Publishing House.

Andrews, E. D., & Torrey, R. A. (2016). *Christian Living: How to Succeed in the Christian Life.* Cambridge, OH: Christian Publishing House.

Andrews, S. J., & Bergen, R. D. (2009). *Holman Old Testament Commentary: 1-2 Samuel.* Nashville: Broadman & Holman.

D., A. E. (2017). *ANGELS & DEMONS: The Bible Answers.* Cambridge, OH: Christian Publishing House.

D., A. E. (2022). *THE RISE OF CATHOLICISM: The Great Apostasy.* Cambridge, OH: Christian Publishing House.

Marshall, T. F., & Andrews, E. D. (2022). *PAUL'S LETTER TO THE PHILIPPIANS: An Apologetic and Background Exposition of the Holy Scriptures.* Cambridge, Ohio: Christian publishing House.

Ryken, L., & Andrews, E. D. (2026). *WILLIAM TYNDALE'S NEW TESTAMENT: A Biography of the Book that Changed Our World.* Cambridge, Ohio: Christian Publishing House.

HUMAN IMPERFECTION

www.ingramcontent.com/pod-product-compliance
Lightning Source LLC
Chambersburg PA
CBHW022106040426
42451CB00007B/147